PrestaShop 1.3 Theming

Beginner's Guide

Develop flexible, powerful, and professional themes for your PrestaShop store through simple steps

Hayati Hashim

BIRMINGHAM - MUMBAI

PrestaShop 1.3 Theming
Beginner's Guide

First published: July 2010

Production Reference: 1160710

Published by Packt Publishing Ltd.
32 Lincoln Road
Olton
Birmingham, B27 6PA, UK.

ISBN 978-1-849511-72-8

www.packtpub.com

Cover Image by Duraid Fatouhi (duraidfatouhi@yahoo.com)

Credits

Author
Hayati Hashim

Reviewers
Adrian Nethercott
Bart Sallé

Acquisition Editor
Dilip Venkatesh

Development Editor
Wilson D'souza

Technical Editor
Sakina Kaydawala

Copy Editor
Leonard D'Silva

Indexer
Monica Ajmera Mehta

Editorial Team Leader
Aanchal Kumar

Project Team Leader
Lata Basantani

Project Coordinator
Shubhanjan Chatterjee

Proofreader
Lesley Harrison

Graphics
Geetanjali Sawant

Production Coordinator
Arvindkumar Gupta

Cover Work
Arvindkumar Gupta

About the Author

Hayati Hashim, graduated from the Queensland University, Australia and later pursued her Masters Degree in Multimedia majoring in e-Learning technologies from Multimedia University, Malaysia. Her latest field of interest is related to mobile learning and applications. She currently manages a multimedia company, Pixel Bytes Sdn Bhd, which offers video, web and multimedia services. She works mostly on open source platforms and has trained students in multimedia, web design, development, e-learning, and e-commerce projects. She loves science fiction movies, reading, painting, photography, travelling, and especially enjoys playing online games, although she hardly gets her hands on them, as this is the way she finds inspiration. This is her first book.

Throughout the progress of writing this book, I have also learned and been assisted by many individuals who deserved special acknowledgements. It is an impossible effort without the tremendous support of the Packt editorial team. There are times when I got swamped with other commitments, work, and family matters, but all of you have certainly kept me motivated to complete it.

I would also like to thank the reviewers (Adrian and Bart) for their constructive feedback throughout the review process. This book would never have been the same if it wasn't for your invaluable feedback and comments.

Special thanks to my beloved husband and son, who supported me all the way and continuously inspired me in my pursuit. This is also to my beloved mother and in the memory of my late father.

About the Reviewers

Adrian Nethercott, born in Australia, has had an interest in computers since he was introduced to them in primary school, where he was chosen as computer monitor. In high school, he studied computers and business and won subject awards for Computer Studies, Accounting, and Business Communications and Technology. He continued his study at James Cook University and completed a Bachelor of Information Technology with Honors' Class I, the highest possible class. For two years, he continued studying for a PhD in Information Technology before deciding that he would rather create websites than do research.

Adrian then worked for three months at Charleville State High School where he redesigned and maintained their Joomla! website. Shortly after, he started working at NQ Web Design, a professional website design company, where he was introduced to PrestaShop. After working there for 15 months, he decided to leave the job and start his own website development company, Nethercott Constructions. He has now been working with PrestaShop for 18 months and is a moderator on the PrestaShop forums under his nickname "Rocky". He has created a website for Nethercott Constructions where he presents a portfolio of websites he has done and offers PrestaShop modules for sale. In the future, he plans to create more PrestaShop modules and a PrestaShop desktop client that will make maintaining PrestaShop websites easier.

I would like to thank my girlfriend Emma-Jane and my parents for their love and support.

After several jobs in the IT sector, **Bart Sallé** discovered the fascinating world of web design. What started as a hobby soon grew to a successful company. His skills increased from web design to web development (PHP and Typoscript).

Now, after several years, he produces high quality products, based on open source software.

Bart Sallé is a specialist in Typo3, Joomla (/Virtuemart), Wordpress, OS-Commerce, and PrestaShop.

His company website can be found at www.os-solutions.nl

His personal site website can be found at www.bartsalle.nl

Table of Contents

Preface

The fitting elements of digital design can make or break websites. In an e-commerce site, creating a convincing theme to support your online store makes valuable impact to your business. Customers or site visitors are the centre to the design of any e-commerce site. He/she may not know much about your company and the products or services it sells, yet he's/she's faced with the information presented on the website to make a buying decision. The personality of the web pages must be perceived as the "face" of the company or the store which gives the visitor anticipation, enticing him/her to further explore the web store. Whether you are a web developer hired to design a PrestaShop store or the owner of the store, this book will guide you on how to create new themes or modify the outlook of your PrestaShop store according to your needs.

PrestaShop is a professional e-commerce shopping cart software, which is free and easily downloadable online. It has been released under the Open Software License v3.0 (http://www.opensource.org/licenses/osl-3.0.php).

According to the official PrestaShop website, "it was built to take advantage of essential Web 2.0 innovations such as dynamic AJAX-powered features and next-generation ergonomy."

PrestaShop considers the usability aspect where users are guided in a manner they can navigate through the e-commerce site and browse a catalog "intelligently and effortlessly", resulting into higher conversion rates from site visitors to paying customers.

The PrestaShop developer prided the software as "lightweight and speedy", which is an advantage to customers with low connection speeds. This is an important feature as Internet connectivity can still be an issue and affect a customer's experience in an online store.

PrestaShop is also user friendly both to the merchant (having a friendly back office administration) and the site visitors/prospective customers, as you will see later.

Although PrestaShop is currently designed as single shop software, where it isn't possible to feature multiple shops on one site, one of its greatest advantages is multi-user administration, where a shop owner may have a few levels of administrators to assist him with managing the online store. This feature is useful in the situation where an online store owner wants someone to assist him with updating information on his product lines featuring new sales or uploading images of new stock.

With the many winning features for functionality and ease of use, PrestaShop is also easier to style than most e-commerce software. The PrestaShop theme is a packaged file that controls the look and feel of the PrestaShop store. It enables site owners or developers to build a visually appealing site that matches the concept of the product or service the store sells.

Through a good choice of themes, site developers may create a more convincing e-commerce site for their customers, allowing them to better present or showcase their products or catalogs.

As with any other similar platform where design and the information are separated, the theme is the utmost important package that can be considered as the backbone that makes up a PrestaShop store.

An effective website will have to consider a few key elements, which include being visually attractive, presenting meaningful information and providing ease of navigation.

This book is dedicated to those who want to change and modify their PrestaShop's default theme to suit their needs and also to build a new theme using the simplest methods.

As theming is also affected by the use of modules and certain effects such as animated images this book will also guide you with tips to make your site unique by employing some of the available techniques.

What this book covers

Chapter 1, Customizing PrestaShop gives a brief introduction to PrestaShop; it will explain the relationship between the PrestaShop front page look and its back office administration, and it will brief you on the basic structure diagram of a PrestaShop theme. It will then give an overview of the back office tabs for modifying the PrestaShop's theme.

Chapter 2, Customizing PrestaShop Theme Part I covers the ways to modify the general layout of the PrestaShop's theme. Here, you will be guided on editing the theme and playing around with the modules. You will get to know terms such as hooks, transplanting, and positioning.

Chapter 3, Customizing PrestaShop Theme Part 2 helps you in setting up your key elements such as the title, header, footer, logos and so on, which complete the look of the store you are designing.

Chapter 4, *Adjusting Style Sheets* helps you understand and review your themes CSS files—modifying the elements of your PrestaShop web pages in terms of the colors, fonts, and layout by making simple changes to the relevant code.

Chapter 5, *Applying Images* elaborates about getting and using images to complete the look of the theme for the online store.

Chapter 6, *Steps for Creating Themes* covers the process of creating a theme step-by-step. It is divided into sub-topics, which are visualizing your theme, color scheming, developing raw materials, getting the layout you want, deciding on what modules you want to use, positioning the modules, customizing categories, adjusting the style sheets, and packaging the theme.

Chapter 7, *Tips and Tricks to Make PrestaShop Theming Easier* explores tips and tricks on how to make it easier to develop themes. It also explains ways to use third party modules for PrestaShop theming.

Chapter 8, *Deploying Your New Themes* explains how to deploy the themes on a production site and how to validate the code and test it on various browsers.

What you need for this book

You will need the following:

- ◆ PrestaShop software (current version v1.3.1). Have it installed on the computer or a hosted server which you can access using FTP or cPanel. You can download it from `www.prestashop.com`.
- ◆ Firefox, the browser we will use for web development, can be downloaded from `http://www.mozilla.com/en-US/`
- ◆ Web developer tools for Firefox, such as Firebugs and Web Developer extension.
- ◆ Notepad or a similar source code editor or Dreamweaver. Notepad can be downloaded from `http://notepad-plus-plus.org/`.

Who this book is for

This book is meant for beginners to PrestaShop who want a hassle-free way to come up with their own themes. If you are a designer who enjoys creative works but does not want to spend too much time exploring the code, this book is for you. This book is also useful for those "layman" online store owners, who want to make their own modifications to their PrestaShop stores.

Conventions

In this book, you will find a number of styles of text that distinguish between different kinds of information. Here are some examples of these styles, and an explanation of their meaning.

Code words in text are shown as follows: "Try changing the `background-color`."

A block of code is set as follows:

```
*, body{margin:0;padding:0}
#maintenance
{
  width:450px;
  margin:35px auto 0 auto;
  padding:12px 0;
  background:#fff;
  text-align:center;
  text-transform:none;
  font-weight:normal;
  letter-spacing:0;
  color: #C73178;
}
```

When we wish to draw your attention to a particular part of a code block, the relevant lines or items are set in bold:

```
#maintenance
{
  width:750px;
  margin:35px auto 0 auto;
  padding:12px 0;
  background:#fefefe;
  text-align:center;
  text-transform:none;
  font-weight:bold;
  letter-spacing:0;
  color: #3FCA66;
}
```

New terms and **important words** are shown in bold. Words that you see on the screen, in menus or dialog boxes for example, appear in the text like this: "Click on the **Save** button".

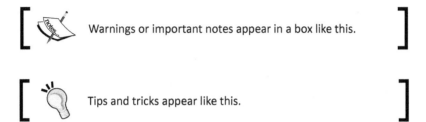

Warnings or important notes appear in a box like this.

Tips and tricks appear like this.

Reader feedback

Feedback from our readers is always welcome. Let us know what you think about this book— what you liked or may have disliked. Reader feedback is important for us to develop titles that you really get the most out of.

To send us general feedback, simply send an e-mail to feedback@packtpub.com, and mention the book title via the subject of your message.

If there is a book that you need and would like to see us publish, please send us a note in the **SUGGEST A TITLE** form on www.packtpub.com or e-mail suggest@packtpub.com.

If there is a topic that you have expertise in and you are interested in either writing or contributing to a book on, see our author guide on www.packtpub.com/authors.

Customer support

Now that you are the proud owner of a Packt book, we have a number of things to help you to get the most from your purchase.

Downloading the example code for the book

You can download the example code files for all Packt books you have purchased from your account at http://www.PacktPub.com. If you purchased this book elsewhere, you can visit http://www.PacktPub.com/support and register to have the files e-mailed directly to you.

Errata

Although we have taken every care to ensure the accuracy of our content, mistakes do happen. If you find a mistake in one of our books—maybe a mistake in the text or the code—we would be grateful if you would report this to us. By doing so, you can save other readers from frustration and help us improve subsequent versions of this book. If you find any errata, please report them by visiting http://www.packtpub.com/support, selecting your book, clicking on the **let us know** link, and entering the details of your errata. Once your errata are verified, your submission will be accepted and the errata will be uploaded on our website, or added to any list of existing errata, under the Errata section of that title. Any existing errata can be viewed by selecting your title from http://www.packtpub.com/support.

Piracy

Piracy of copyright material on the Internet is an ongoing problem across all media. At Packt, we take the protection of our copyright and licenses very seriously. If you come across any illegal copies of our works, in any form, on the Internet, please provide us with the location address or website name immediately so that we can pursue a remedy.

Please contact us at copyright@packtpub.com with a link to the suspected pirated material.

We appreciate your help in protecting our authors, and our ability to bring you valuable content.

Questions

You can contact us at questions@packtpub.com if you are having a problem with any aspect of the book, and we will do our best to address it

1
Customizing PrestaShop

Just like in any bricks-and-mortar retail business, an online store will have a shop front or a display area and a back-of-house area where the administration activities and management of business is carried out. For online businesses, the pages that appear on your customers' browser are your shop front. In PrestaShop, we will refer this as your front office. Your back-of-house area will be your PrestaShop's back office administration panel.

For this chapter, we will firstly give you a brief rundown of what skill sets you should have to fully benefit from this book. We will later learn how the PrestaShop back office administration panel affects your theme, which in turn affects what your site visitors will see on their browser.

Now that you have successfully installed the PrestaShop program, you must have noticed that PrestaShop comes with a default template that is ready to be customized.

Let's then get to the business of understanding this default template. This will allow you to change the layout and the look of your online shop. Later you will even be able to build your own themes.

As you progress, you will realize that you may execute things differently to get the same result. You may also work on the FTP or the hosting where you "tweak" the scripts on the servers.

What you need to know

As this book is geared towards beginners who have little knowledge of scripting and hardcoding of markup languages, we will explain the steps visually. To be able to maximize the benefit of the book, you absolutely need to have the following:

◆ PrestaShop installed and configured correctly: You will need PrestaShop installed on either your localhost or your webserver. This book is based on version 1.3. You should be able to download the latest version at `http://www.PrestaShop.com/en/downloads`. Being familiar with the backend is not a prerequisite, as we will be covering that later.

If you are new to PrestaShop, get the information on how to install it from `http://www.PrestaShop.com/wiki/Installing_And_Updating_PrestaShop_Software/`

◆ You will need a Notepad or another editor for HTML. You may also choose any editor you wish. A more expensive option would be to purchase Dreamweaver.

Other free editors can be obtained at a number of sites such as:
`http://www.pnotepad.org/`
`http://notepad-plus.sourceforge.net/uk/site.htm`
`http://www.crimsoneditor.com/`
`http://www.pspad.com`

◆ You should also have access to the FTP of the installation and backend access to the administration panel. If you used a third party to host your PrestaShop, you will have to ask them to have it installed. Most webhosting companies already have PrestaShop as one of the e-commerce options and it can be installed through a number of auto installers such as Softaculous Premium, or Installatron. You only need to upload the PrestaShop program to a new directory in the public HTML or a sub-directory. It can be installed easily by accessing this new directory (for example, `www.yourdomain.com` or `www.yourdomain.com/prestas`) through your browser and then following a few simple steps to complete the installation.

◆ An understanding of W3C's requirement for a table-less layout: PrestaShop uses a convention that meets the W3C's requirements for a table-less layout. Therefore, it is important to have an understanding on how this works in order to develop the new themes.

W3C's website: www.w3.org/

- XHTML and CSS: Most development of new themes can be done without knowledge of XHTML or CSS, as there are plenty of What You See Is What You Get (WYSIWYG) editors that allow the flexibility of designing without the coding knowledge. However, understanding them is useful in developing better themes that can be more efficient and load better. Through this understanding, you may also make the themes Search Engine Optimization (SEO) friendly. After all, there is no point having pretty looking web pages that cannot be found by your prospective visitors.

 Learn about CSS at: http://www.w3schools.com/css/default.asp
XHTML at: http://www.w3schools.com/xhtml/default.asp
and Smarty at: http://www.smarty.net/docs.php

- Web developer tools such as Firebug or the Web Developer extension for Firefox. Download Web Developer extension at: http://www.chrispederick.com/work/web-developer/. You can also use Firebug, which is one of the most popular web development tools, and is available at http://www.getfirebug.com.

- A knowledge of image editing as you will be required to create themes based on what wants to be projected through the concept of the themes, for example, suitable color schemes for icons used if you plan to develop your own unique themes. You will also need this knowledge to edit images you have captured, for example, the showcased products.

 To expedite, you may want to subscribe to Stockphoto and icons available on the net as resources, for example, www.istockphoto.com, www.deviantart.com, http://www.sxc.hu/ are popular royalty free image distributors that you can use for a low fee.

Getting familiar with PrestaShop

The reason why it is important that you have those basics clear is that it will make it much easier to understand what can be done to modify the theme. However, if you knew everything, you wouldn't need a beginner's book. We do not expect you to be at an intermediate or an advanced level; this beginner's book will show you step by step how to modify the default theme and develop a new theme for your online shop.

For a start, let's look at the default theme named "PrestaShop" that comes in the PrestaShop software pack.

The PrestaShop sample sites

Let's have a look at a few example of sites that have been developed using PrestaShop. There are many nicely built sites, which are drawn out of using just the default themes. Some use more additional third party modules, which helped make a more unique look, for example, using a top menu bar, moving boxes on the featured block, and so on.

Let's have a look at a few sites we have chosen as examples:

◆ `http://www.Homology.com`—Using "carousels" for products and footer links, the designer has also managed to make a unique look.

◆ `http://www.peugeotsport-store.com/`—An example of a minimalistic approach in changing the default theme but the end result is good. Here, the designer maintained the three columns of the default template and played around keeping a limited color on the blocks and integrated a flash file at the home page center column.

◆ `http://www.dakoyo.fr`—This site is also using the three column layout, just like the default theme. There is a use of flash slide in the home page center column, and the image gallery viewer does make a lot of difference, even if most of the basic structure is retained.

◆ http://www.lookforlook.com—By changing the home page logo picture with a flash slide show, a "carousel" on featured products, and using a top menu bar, a footer, and so on, the theme looks very different from the default theme.

You can view more of these on the PrestaShop website in the live showcases section.

Time for action—Overviewing the back office administration panel

Let's get familiar with the basics of the PrestaShop back office administration that relates to the theming of the shop front or front office of your PrestaShop store.

Now, using the default theme in PrestaShop, have a look at your current storefront and how the theme is governed by the back office control. By looking at this, you can tell which back office item you need to modify, replace, or set according to your needs.

Basically, the layout can be seen here in the following screenshot:

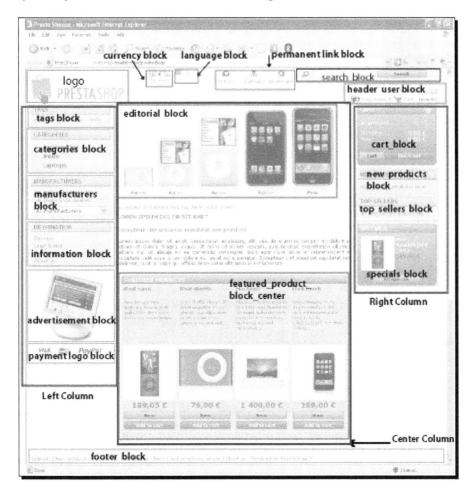

Now this is how your back office administration panel, which controls these blocks, should look. The default theme has three columns (left, center, and right columns). Each column comprises a number of blocks which are moveable. For example, within the **Right Column**, there are **cart_block**, **new products block**, **top seller block**, and **specials block**. These blocks can be displayed within the left block as well. We also have a **header user** and **footer block** where you can install blocks for a number of modules.

Next, we will look at the back office, as shown in the following screenshot:

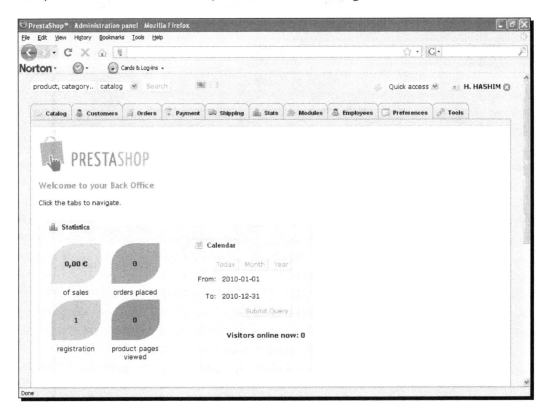

There are ten tabs, which are named **Catalog**, **Customers**, **Orders**, **Payment**, **Shipping**, **Stats**, **Modules**, **Employees**, **Preferences**, and **Tools**.

They are all important and useful if you know how to manipulate them to improve the efficiency of your store's administration and operation. However, to modify your store theme, just a few of them will be necessary and we will get an overview of those here.

The tabs in the back office that control the look of your shop are:

1. **Preferences**
2. **Modules**

3. **Catalog**

4. **Tools**

Preferences

The most important tab, when it comes to modifying the default theme, is probably the Preferences tab. Go to **Back Office | Preferences**, and you will see something like the following screenshot. This is the **Preferences** landing page, which is also referred to as **General.**

You will see a few things, such as the following:

- **PrestaShop directory**—This is where the default directory is located in your server. It can be blank if the default directory is at the root of your public HTML folder, whereas, in the example, a new directory named **prestash** was created when installing the software.

- **Enable Shop**—You set the enable or the activated state for your shop or if it is already deactivated.

- **Maintenance IP**—You specify the **IP address allowed to access the Front Office even if the shop is disabled.**

- **Enable SSL**—Enabled or disabled depending on **If your hosting provider allows SSL, you can activate SSL encryption (https://) for customer account identification and order processing.**

- **Increase Front Office security**—This states, **Enable or disable token on the Front Office in order to improve PrestaShop security**

- **Friendly URL**—Enable only if your server allows URL rewriting (recommended). This feature will require a creation of an .htaccess file.

- **Back Office help boxes**—Enable yellow help boxes which are displayed under form fields in the Back Office. This can be set to yes or no.

- **Terms of service**—When you design the site, you need to decide if customers are required to accept or decline terms of service before their order will be processed. Terms of service are used to prevent legal problems.

- **Offer gift-wrapping**—If you enable this, gift-wrapping suggestions will be offered to the customer, and the customer will be able to leave a message to be printed alongside the order.

- **Gift-wrapping price**—This sets a price for gift-wrapping.

- **Gift-wrapping tax**—This sets a tax for gift wrapping.

- **Offer recycled-packaging**—If you like, you can also suggest recycled packaging to customer.

- **Cart re-display at login**—If enabled, the contents of the user's last shopping cart will be recalled and displayed upon the next time the user logs in.

- **Round mode**—You can choose the rounding of prices, rounding always superior, inferior or classical rounding.

- **Automatically check updates to modules**—New modules and updates are displayed on module page.

- **Timezone**—You can also set the timezone of the store. Currently, it is quite exhaustive, and includes almost every available zone such as Africa, America, Asia, Europe, Pacific, Australia, Chile, Indian, Canadan and the GMT, PST, and so on.

- **v1.1 theme compatibility**—If enabled, the shop will use a PrestaShop v1.1 theme (SSL will generate warnings in the customer's browser).

Although most of these are not directly related to your theme development mission, it is useful to know some of the key options and tabs that make PrestaShop work.

Next, the **Preferences** tab comprises the settings controlling the sub-items, which we will briefly explain as follows:

♦ **Contact**: Go to **Back Office | Preferences | Contact**. Here you will get to set the **Shop name**, **Shop e-mail** which will be used to contact the administrator, you can fill in your shop **Registration** information here, along with the **Shop address**, **Country**, **Phone**, and **Fax** number. However, the only required fields are the top two, that is, the **Shop name** and the **Shop e-mail** address.

♦ **Appearance**: The sub items in the **Appearance** section are for selecting your **Header logo** and **Favicon**. This is the most important stub to control the appearance of your site. Click on **Back Office | Preferences | Appearance | Themes** and you can see the thumbnail of the theme applied to your shop. By default, we only have one theme choice, that is, **prestashop**. If you have more than one theme installed, you will see more thumbnails next to the default theme. You will be able to change the **Header logo** and **Favicon** through this tab as well.

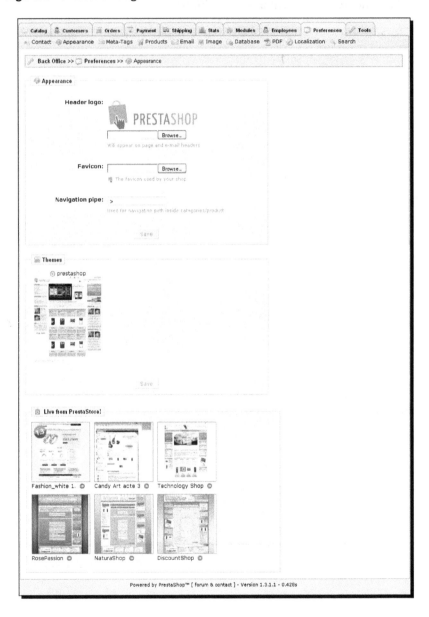

If you have added a new theme, it will be displayed next to the PrestaShop theme thumbnail in the **Themes** section, as shown in the preceding screenshot. For PrestaShop 1.3 and above, a new item is added on this page where a link **Live from PrestaStore!** is provided for purchasing readymade themes.

◆ **Meta-Tags**: Click on each of the "edit" icons (the pencil-like icon on the right) and edit the meta tags of each page. If you need to add a new meta tag for a different page, just add a new page and proceed with editing the page title, meta description, and meta keywords.

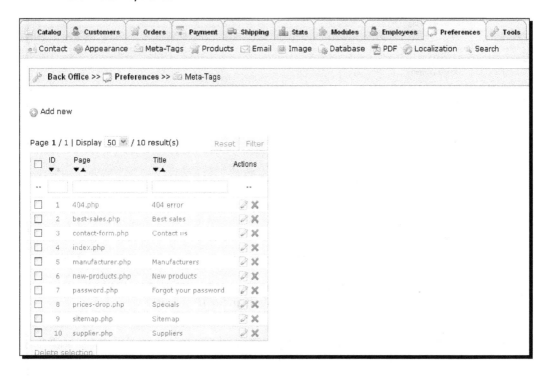

◆ **Products**: The **Products** sub tab is important as it sets how the products are featured on your store. Here you can choose how your products are displayed in the front office.

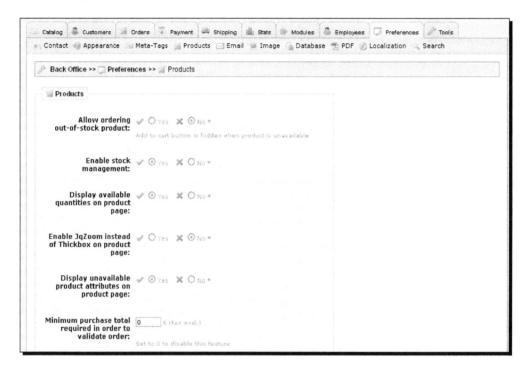

◆ **Email**: Use this setting to determine how the e-mails are sent by the back office (through the PHPmail() function or through an SMTP server).

◆ **Image**: This can be used to customize the different sizes used by PrestaShop to display your images and regenerate all your thumbnails.

Here, the next action will be to either add a new type of thumbnail, and set the width and height of it, or you can edit the existing thumbnails (for example, small, medium, and so on) and decide which type of thumbnails (to refer the thumbnail and specific height and width of each type of thumbnails) should be applied to either **Products**, **Categories**, **Manufactures**, **Suppliers**, and **Scenes**.

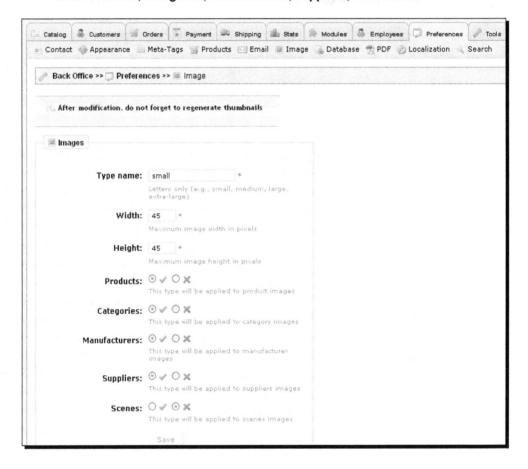

- ◆ **Database**: This sub-item sets the server, database, prefix, username, and password. This is related to the `config/settings.inc.php` file. This configures the connection settings between PrestaShop and its MySQL database.

- ◆ **PDF**: The **PDF** sub-item sets the encoding for any PDF invoices and the font used in the PDF invoices. The language setting by default is **English**.

- ◆ **Localization**: Strangely, the **Localization** sub-item only allows you to specify the **weight** unit of the store. In most cases the weight unit will be **kg**.

◆ **Search**: The **Search** setting allow site visitor to search for words which are based on your configuration here. For example, if you're looking for "a large box of dark chocolate", it will only search for "large" and "chocolate", as the other words are less commonly searched for Depending on this configuration setting, you can set the minimum word length to be two characters, as the value three means that only words of four characters or longer, whereas the value two allows the user to search for three character words.

Catalog

The next important tab would be the **Catalog** attributes.

The **Catalog** comprises the controlling tab for the categories and products you are showcasing in your store. In this tab, you will have a number of sub-items that will require you to key in data. This tab controls a number of modules as well, such as the **CATEGORIES** block and the **FEATURED PRODUCTS** block. We will explore this in more detail in *Chapter 3, Customizing PrestaShop Theme Part 2*.

- **Tracking** provides a snapshot of what is empty, disabled, and out of stock categories.
- **Manufacturers** tab is where you can edit information of their products, add new manufacturers, or insert their logos
- **Suppliers** tab is similar to manufacturers, except that the suppliers' information fields do not include address information like the manufacturers' do.
- **Attributes and groups** tab is where you can find out the attributes of a group. For example, you can add colors as one of the attributes.
- **Features** tab will allow more information to be provided to the visitors for valuable comparison on the products' features.
- **Image mapping** allows a pop-up to appear displaying a brief description of the product when customer hovers over the image with the mouse. When clicked, it opens to the product's full product page. This relates to **Preferences | Image**, which we explained in the previous section where image thumbnails are generated according to the size specified.

It is best if you have some images ready for the product's photo or edited images when working on this.

Modules

This is perhaps the tab where you will do the most work, as this is where you can install or enable the modules to customize your pages according to your needs. This is also where you may decide on the location of the modules within your site pages. We will cover the modules and how to move them around (transplanting, positioning, and moving them within columns and within the pages) in *Chapter 2, Customizing PrestaShop Theme Part I* in greater detail.

The **Modules** tab allows you to control the modules you want to use in the store. You will be able to transplant the modules and move them around according to the site navigation. You can move them up or down of the columns, you may also position them in the left or the right column, and you may disable them.

In the version prior to PrestaShop 1.3, you also have the option whether you want to add a new module or purchase one from the PrestaStore. However, after v1.3 was released, this has been disabled.

The list of the existing modules that are readily available in PrestaShop 1.3.1 are:

1. **Advertisement – 1 module**

2. **Stats Engine – 5 modules**

3. **Products module – 6 modules**

4. **Payment – 8 modules**

5. **Tools – 14 modules**

6. **Blocks – 23 modules**

7. **Stats – 25 modules**

In order to make the modules work, you will have to check if it is installed and enabled. PrestaShop buttons are simple; when you see the **Uninstall** button, which is towards the rightmost portion of each module, it indicates the module has already been installed. If you see a 'tick' next to the installation button, it means that the module is already in the enabled state. Some will need to be configured where **>>Configure** is shown next to the module title and descriptions.

The one that controls the images that appear on your main page can be found at **Modules | Tools | Home text editor v1.5**. All you need to do is make sure it is installed and enabled. By clicking **>>Configure**, you will be taken to a page where you may modify it according to your requirements.

Tools

A number of tools are provided to simplify your task in making your PrestaShop store work. The following explains in brief what each sub-item in the **Tools** tab does:

- **Languages**—This tab is where you set the language interface. The default languages included in the PrestaShop pack are English and French. You can add new languages and set the default language option here.

- **Translations**—Here you can modify translations, import or export language packs, or copy data from one language to another.

- **Tabs**—Here you get to see a list of all the tabs you used in your store's back office admin. It also indicates the parent or child tab. You can add or delete new items here, or move them to the left or right according to your preferences.

- **Quick Accesses**—Here you decide whether to make a page open in a new window or not. This is more for the admin tools.

- **Aliases**—This can be used to assist with searching when a site visitor keys in a particular word. It is particularly useful for items which may be typed in wrongly, but yet you have the product in your listing.

- **Import**—You can efficiently upload categories, products, attributes, customers addresses, suppliers, and manufacturers data in a .CSV file to expedite your logistics.

- **Subdomains**—Cookies are different on each sub domain of your website. If you want to use the same cookie, please add the sub domains used by your shop. The most common is subdomain www.

- ◆ **DB backup**—Back up your files often to make sure you don't lose information if something happens to your hosting.

- ◆ **CMS**—This one is particularly useful in theming, as it is also makes the pages linkable to the modules or buttons you create on your home page. The listing in this CMS relates to the Footer link module. When configuring the Footer link module, links you checked (selected) in the particular module will appear at the bottom of your page in the footer block (if you are using the default theme).

- ◆ **Generators**—This is useful for generating .htaccess and a robot file, especially related to SEO. You need to have access to your server host to create the necessary thing before generating this.

Making the most basic change to the default theme

Let's see what we can do by changing the main images (the centre and the logo), and the background color.

Time for action—Making simple changes to affect look of the store

1. Let's start with replacing the logo and the home page logo using the back office administration page.

2. You will need to upload the image in **Preferences | Appearances.**

3. Go to **Back Office | Modules | Tools | Home text editor v1.5**.

4. Replace the home page logo at the center column by configuring the module.

Now, let's try modifying the blocks. We will:

1. Change the position of the **CATEGORIES** block in the left column.

2. Disable the **FEATURED PRODUCTS** block

3. Change the information in the categories.

In the following screenshot, some of the modules on the right were shifted to the left column and some columns on the right have been disabled or moved up or down. We will explain the way to do this in detail in the next chapter.

If you get into trouble, don't worry. We are just getting familiar with the PrestaShop back office control panel.

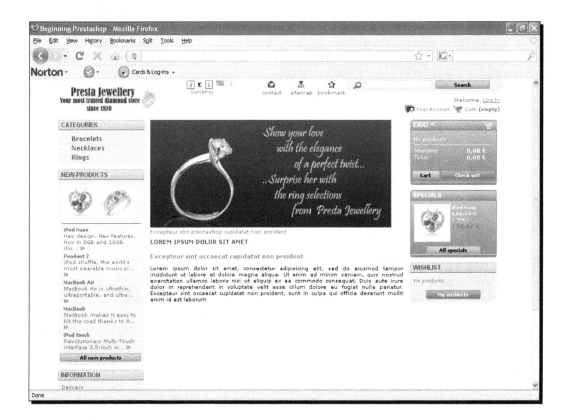

What just happened?

In this section, you have just begun a simple "theming" operation, where one of the essential elements is changing the logo on the top left of the web page. You subsequently started exploring the **Modules** tab as you need to replace the image in the center column. Through the **Modules** tab at the back office panel, you can easily upload the home page logo which is the central editorial image you see in the center column.

To sum up this action, what you have done is simply made a little amendment through the back office tabs and this is probably the easiest way to manipulate the default theme through the site element's consideration. Thus, by making simple changes, you can save a lot of time and still create a fresh looking theme unique to your store.

Have a go hero—Changing looks through simple CSS editing

Now, let's see how modifying the CSS can give a different look and feel to your page. The easiest way to review how the colors change is through online modification with the web developer tools for Firefox such as Web Developer Add-ons or Firebug.

For the Web Developer extension, go to **Tools | Web Developer | Information | Display Element Information**. Then move the mouse over the elements you may want to change and see what needs to be changed, and for Firebug, go to **Tools | Firebug | Inspect Element**.

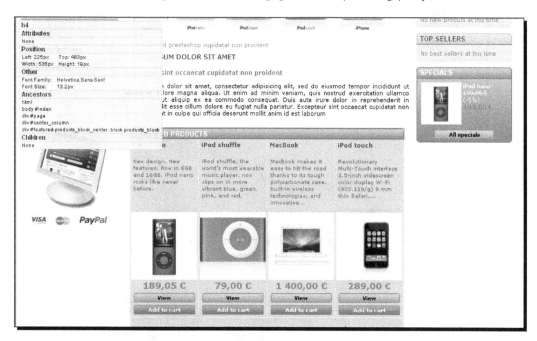

If you want to work on the CSS file, you will need to go to **Tools | Web Developer | CSS | Edit CSS**, and it will be shown on your left split pane.

It is possible to edit a line from the `global.css` file and change the background color from `white` to `blue` to see the change on your browser. Try changing the `background-color` to `blue`, as shown in the following code

```
body {
    background-color: blue;
    font-size: 11px;
    font-family: Verdana, Arial, Helvetica, Sans-Serif;
    color: #5d717e;
    text-align:center
}
```

The following screenshot is what you will see on your browser when you use the Web Developer extension to find out how the website looks when you change the background color to blue.

Alternatively, you can also use Firebug and view the same element edited, as shown in the following screenshot:

As an example, using Firebug the item being pointed to is the **FEATURED PRODUCTS** block, which is highlighted by a blue border. You can see the HTML and CSS scripts at the bottom-left pane, whereas on the bottom-right pane you can see the style used for the element, which is `#center_column div.block h4`.

Try it out for yourself now. Let's try changing the background color of the website. Choose any website, and you can activate your Firebug or use the Web Developer extension tool.

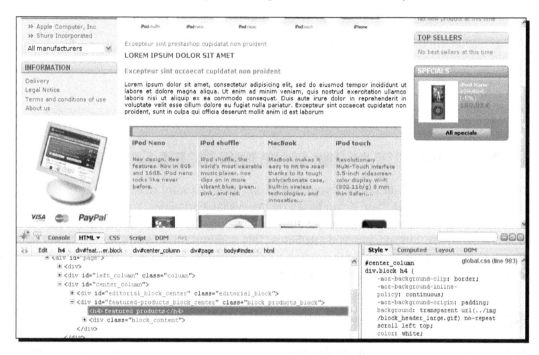

You can choose any of the web developer tools to work with, whichever you are more comfortable with, although the majority of the web developers use Firebug. I used both, but I found Firebug very handy.

You can play around further to look at the possible changes in the look of your PrestaShop site, by modifying the colors of the other elements, but as you can see, there will be more steps in order to change the color of the blocks, the borders, and the fonts. Changing the colors will require a bit more of CSS know-how plus getting the right combination of colors in your scheme. This knowledge of using the Firebug or other similar web developer tools is priceless when it comes to web development or web designing. We will discuss this in greater detail in a specific chapter pertaining to modifying your web elements in terms of color and background images.

Pop quiz

1. How can you navigate to change the image at the center column editorial block or the home page logo through your Back Office?

   a. **Preferences | Appearance**

   b. **Modules | Tools | Block**

   c. **Catalog | Categories**

2. What are the Firefox extensions that we learned to use to edit the theme files?

   a. Firebug

   b. Smarty

   c. CSS

Planning for your online store new theme design

Now, based on the default theme layout, decide on what you want to use in your e-commerce site and list them down based on the available modules. You will also need some dummy data, that is, images of a number of products from a few categories, name of a few manufacturers, pricing, and attributes. This is important for you when you want to develop the site speedily. You don't need to be very accurate, as you may always change your blocks and modules, but it will make it easier later.

Summary

In order to make changes to the default template or develop themes in PrestaShop, you will need to know the basics of this powerful platform.

Getting familiar with how to modify the default theme will enable you to start working on building new themes from scratch.

Specifically, we covered:

- The prerequisites of PrestaShop theming
- The parts in the back office administration that will affect the theming process.

Now that we've learned about the functions of the parts, let's move on to learn about how you can start modifying your store and start building the right look for it. In the next chapter, we will learn more about the module blocks. Knowing how to enable, configure, and understand the module blocks will help you in your theming task.

2
Customizing PrestaShop Theme Part I

Now that we have explored the PrestaShop theming control panel, it's time to move on to the next step. The most basic level is using the back office panel to customize the layout. Using this knowledge, we can make some quick and easy changes without having any technical knowledge.

If you need more advanced changes than what can be achieved here, you will need to edit the theme and the CSS files, which will be explained in the chapters on customizing the theme files later.

It must be noted that all design changes that you can do in this back office can also be achieved through customization on the theme files (which involves editing of the file's markup) too. Although knowledge of this theme editing approach encased that of the back office setting, it is useful to know that there are reasons to choose the latter option with no "hacking" of scripts even if you are an advanced user as there could be some issues when you have to update to the next PrestaShop version. You will have to update some of these modified files as these changes may not be automatically included in the newer version.

Let's now start with our next step.

We have to decide what kind of layout we would want, just like the interior design space of a building that you are erecting, you need to visualize the spaces and how users will navigate your retail outlet.

You will also need to know what kind of resources can help the successful function of your store, customers in real brick-and-mortar stores do not have to ask a lot of questions as they are prone to browsing the items while having the advantage of feeling, smelling, holding, or trying the items at the same time. While this is true for a real store/shop, the online store does not have this advantage. So, consider features/functions that can be a "replacement" to this disadvantage, such as a 30 day return policy.

In a real shop, customers may ask questions at the customer service desks. The same thing can be done with your online store; you can add a lot of information that your customers may need while balancing it with a good design, navigation, and browsing experience. This will ensure that the customer finds the information and this reduces the need to repetitively answer the same queries. This is one of the main reasons why an online store exists, which means that information can be obtained easily 24x7.

Therefore, in an online shop, you will have to decide on what kind of features you want to introduce, for example, one block for product information, another for customer service information where they can get information on return policy, how to make payment, and so on.

This is just a background that is needed to decide the functions of your store. We will not be discussing about what makes a good navigation or whether one way can be more effective than another. We will learn about how you can use the knowledge about theming for PrestaShop-based stores to build your online store or if you are a web designer, your clients' online stores suitable with the stores' concepts. You will also learn how to go about in applying the necessary modules to complement your theme setup.

Before we start this chapter, you should get acquainted with the back office panel. This will help you understand what we are exploring here.

In this chapter, we will be sticking with the default PrestaShop theme and learn how to:

- Install, uninstall, enable, and disable module blocks in the center, left, and right columns.
- Transplant and position modules by moving them to columns and within the columns.

The default layout

Let's have a look again at your current storefront and how the theme is governed by the back office control panel.

By looking at the screenshot, you can tell which back office items you need to modify, replace, or set according to your needs.

The basic layout outline can be seen in the following screenshot:

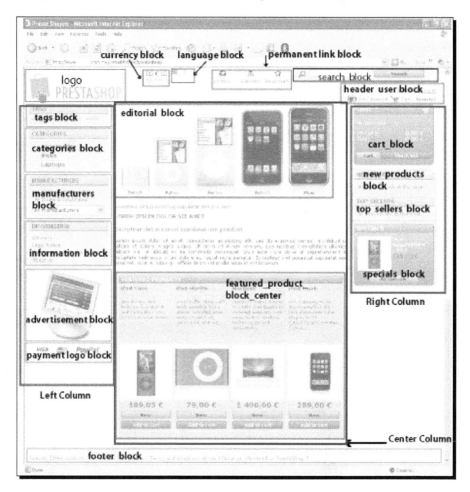

Besides the back office control over appearance, as shown in the previous chapter, our theme is also affected by the modules that control the functionality of your store. At this stage, we will be working on the existing modules in PrestaShop. This is where you decide whether your site visitor will see the product categories, the top selling products, your product listing, the specials, your featured products, and so on. If you run an e-commerce store with a payment option that links automatically to a payment gateway, you may want to study a bit more about each of these modules as well.

You will also notice that the default theme uses a three column layout with a header in the top block and a footer at the bottom. Through the back office panel, all the default blocks on the left and right columns can be moved or transplanted interchangeably.

Some of the blocks in the header (top blocks) can be moved into the left column or right column. The **featured product block** and the **editorial block**, which are at the center column, are pretty much stuck in this position.

Modules

The Modules tab allows you to control the modules you want to use in the store. You will be able to transplant the modules and move them around according to the site navigation you want, considering some limitations at this stage. You can move them up or down in the columns. You may also position them in the left or the right column or you may disable them. You also have the option of adding a new module or choosing ones that are available from the PrestaStore. PrestaShop has some already installed modules, and the number of newly developed ones is growing every day.

Now let's move on to **Back Office | Modules**, as shown in the following screenshot:

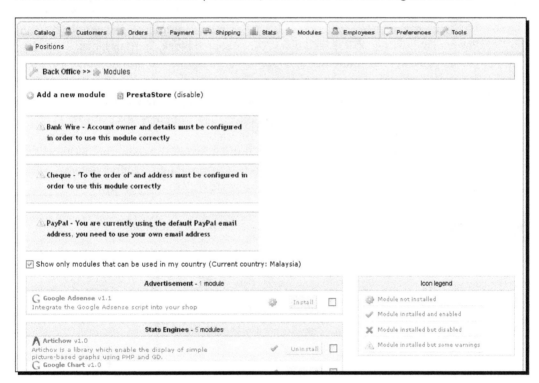

We will go into the listing and get some ideas on each one. However, we will focus in greater detail on the modules that affect theming directly.

Among the existing modules in this version (PrestaShop 1.3.1), which are readily available for installation, some of them are:

1. Advertisement – 1 module: Google Adsense.

2. Products module – 6 modules: Cross selling, RSS products feed, Products Comments, Products Category, Product tooltips, Send to a Friend module.

3. Stats Engines – 5 modules: Artichow, Google Chart, Visifire, XML/SWF Charts, ExtJS.

4. Payment – 8 modules: Bank Wire, Cash on delivery (COD), Cheque, Google Checkout, Hipay, Moneybookers, Paypal, PaypalAPI.

5. Tools – 14 modules (but only 12 modules listed): Birthday Present, Canonical URL, Home text editor, Customers follow-up, Google sitemap, Featured Products on the homepage, Customers loyalty and rewards, Mail alerts, Newsletter, Customer referral program, SMS Tm4b, and Watermark.

6. Blocks – 23 modules: Block advertising, Top seller block, Cart block, Categories block, Currency block, Info block, Language block, Link block, Manufacturers block, My Account block, New products block, Newsletter block, Block payment logo, Permanent links block, RSS feed block, Quick Search block, Specials block, Suppliers block, Tags block, User info block, Footer links block, Viewed products block, Wish list block.

7. Stats – 25 modules: Google Analytics, Pages not found, Search engine keywords, Best categories, Best customers, Best products, Best suppliers, Best vouchers, Carrier distribution, Catalog statistics v1.0, Catalog evaluation, Data mining for statistics, Geolocation, Condensed stats for the Back Office homepage, Visitors online, Newsletter, Visitors origin, Registered Customer Info, Product details, Customer accounts, Sales and orders, Shop search, Visits and Visitors, Tracking - Front office.

You should also see an **Icon legend** on the right that reads the following:

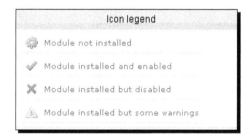

Apart from these three options of installing, enabling, and disabling, you may also add new modules using the button on the top-left corner of the module tab.

There are also plenty of third party modules that can be used to make the store more interactive and attractive. But we will discuss this in *Chapter 7, Tips and Tricks to Make PrestaShop Theming Easier* which covers the tips and tricks to make it easier to set up a different look for your theme.

Time for action—Installing and enabling modules

In order to make the modules work, you will have to check if it is installed and enabled. When you see the word **Install** on the rightmost portion of each module, it indicates the module is yet to be installed. In PrestaShop, when a module is installed, it is automatically enabled.

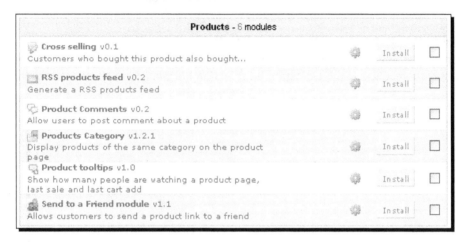

The following screenshot shows an example of the installed and uninstalled states.

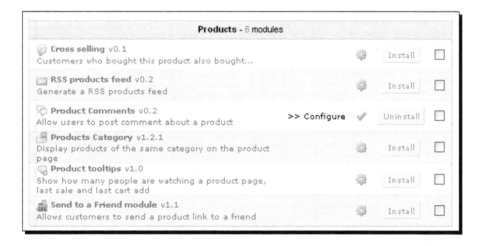

By simply clicking on the **Install** button, we have installed and enabled the modules. Note that some modules will require further configuring, while others work fine automatically once they are installed. The green tick indicates enabled modules.

Have a go hero—Choosing the modules to install

It is best to start with a blank page. So, what we will do now is disable all the modules by clicking the green check button so it will turn into the disabled state again.

When you begin to modify your default setting in PrestaShop, you may want to know how each installation affects your store. It is best to reset the installation to the maximum by disabling modules to avoid confusing yourself.

To make things easier, you can also uninstall them all. This can be done speedily by checking all the modules, which are already installed and go to the bottom of the page of the modules to uninstall them. Click on the **Uninstall the selection** button, and they will be uninstalled.

Don't panic when you get a blank page on your front office. You may only be seeing a blank page plus the logo, which is controlled by another **admin** tab we learned about it in the previous chapter.

Positioning modules

Before we start installing and enabling modules, let's learn two important terms that you need to understand in PrestaShop's modules. They are as follows:

1. Hooks
2. Transplanting

Hooks

A hook is a place where the module code can be inserted. In the back office, hooks are shown in a block that comprises a few modules installed within it. As an example, the right column blocks is a hook, which is like a housing for the four modules (**Cart block**, **New products block**, **Top seller block**, and **Specials block**) as shown in the following screenshot. It is possible to change the order of these modules that have been placed within the hook.

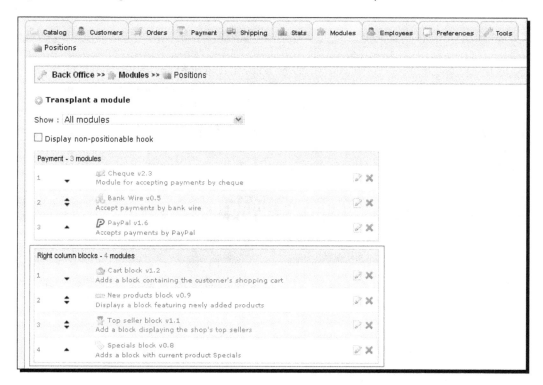

Transplanting modules

Transplanting a module is enabling the module to be displayed in a different hook.

For example, once you have installed and enabled a **New products** module, it will be hooked to the right column, as a default position. When you transplant another **New products** module, you will have to specify where to hook it.

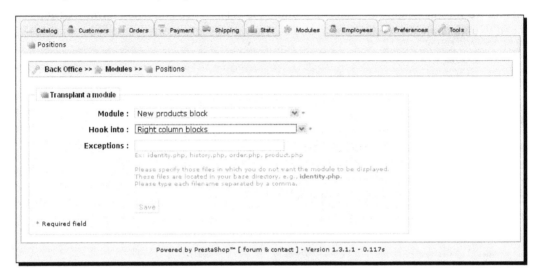

If you transplant another one within the same column (the right column), you will have two of the **New products** modules there. You can also transplant a **New products** module within the left and right column if you want to, but that will not look right.

You need to install a module to be able to transplant it. A disabled module can still be transplanted and moved up or down within a column. It just won't be displayed in the front office. We will go into this in greater detail after we learn more about installing the modules.

Time for action—Installing the Home text editor module

You will note that some modules are automatically set and need little configuring to be able to be used and viewed by the site user.

One of the key modules in the center column, that you will need to work on, is the **Home text editor** module, as shown previously (this was referred to as the **editorial block**). Now, let's get started with installing this module.

1. Go to **Back Office** | **Modules** and scroll down in the **Tools** block.

2. Look for **Home text editor v1.5**.

3. Click on the **Install** button for this module, and click on **>>Configure**. You will get the center block and the text that you may want to edit and configure accordingly. You will see the following:

- ❏ **Main title**
- ❏ **Subheading**
- ❏ **Introductory text**
- ❏ **Homepage's logo**
- ❏ **Homepage logo link**
- ❏ **Homepage logo subheading**

4. The next screenshot shows the default page before it was edited:

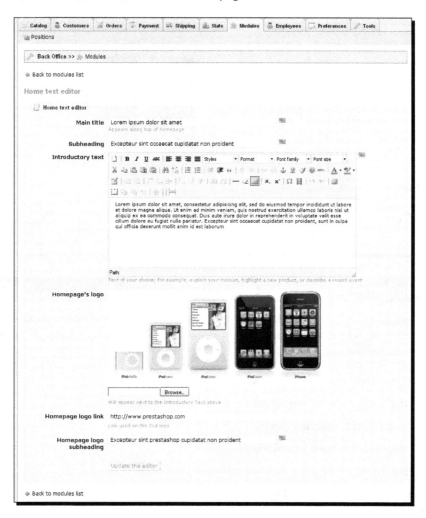

The **Main title** appears at the bottom of the home page logo. It is also set as the **Homepage logo's** alternate tag, not the title tag. It will be displayed when hovering over the image in IE6. In IE7 (and above) and other browsers, it will not be displayed on hovering.

The **Subheading** appears below the **Main title**. It is the **Homepage logo subheading** that appears below the **Homepage's logo**.

The **Introductory text** is the one that will appear at the bottom of the **Subheading**.

The following image shows the relationship between what is affected by the editorial input you keyed in on your home page editor in the back office. The text on the left and right column is annotated to a front office view of a browser to relate the link with the fields you need to fill out in the back office.

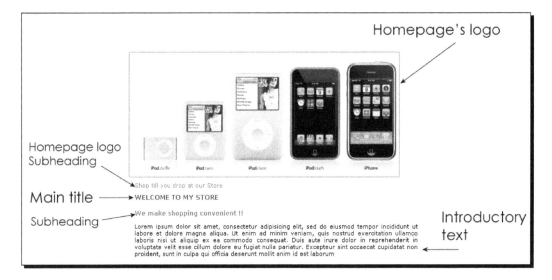

Have a go hero—Adding more blocks

Now that you have installed, enabled, and configured the **Home text editor** module within the center column, let's proceed with adding more blocks on the other parts of the site. You will need to do the following:

1. Decide which other modules we want.

2. Install and enable the modules for the left and right columns.

3. Configure the **Modules** blocks.

4. Transplant and hook the modules.

5. Learn about moving the blocks to different columns.

6. Learn about moving the blocks within columns.

We will go into greater detail about configuring each one of the modules, installed in the next chapter.

Now that you have decided on which modules to add on your website, we will work on one example, namely, the **CATEGORIES** block installation. Once you know how to go about doing this, it will be a breeze, as some of these activities can be quite repetitive and PrestaShop's administration navigation is pretty simple to understand.

Time for action—Installing, enabling, and configuring the Categories block

You will need to install the chosen blocks using the following steps:

1. Go to the **Modules | Blocks |** scroll down and find the **Categories block** just like the **Home text editor** module, which we installed some time back.

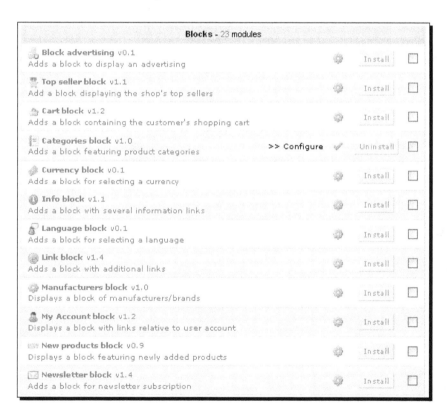

2. Once you have enabled the installed **Categories block**, you will see the block appear in your front office, as shown in the following image:

3. Configure the block. In this case, we will be able to decide how many categories we want to display in our category block.

4. You will get to set the **Maximum depth** of the sublevels displayed in the block.

5. This specifies how many categories you have in your category box. By default, there are three sublevels and the module block is positioned on the top left of your web page.

6. You can also choose the **Dynamic** mode on this sublevel.

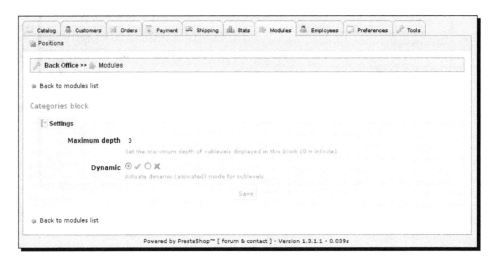

Having the **Maximum depth** of the **Categories block** of 3, you may have the following within your **Categories block**:

- a category
- a sub-category
- a sub-sub-category

This actually relates to the next tab, which is in the **Catalog** tab, and we will cover this tab in the next chapter.

The next screenshot shows what is seen in your **CATEGORIES** block in your front office:

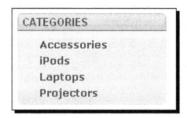

This categorization is mostly common sense and logistically connected to how you want to categorize items in your store.

The **CATEGORIES** block can show such a three parent category, as shown in the preceding screenshot, or with a child category, as shown in the following screenshot:

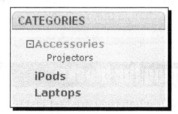

Next, we will install **Top sellers block**, **New products block**, **Cart block**, **Info block**, and a **Newsletter block**. We will see that all these blocks are moveable or transplantable elsewhere in the page. Using this back office function, you will still be limited to moving each of them to either the left or the right column, but not the center column.

Time for action—Moving the modules within the column

There are a few ways to position a module through the PrestaShop back office. This also depends on the expected navigation of your web page. As mentioned, modules are, by default, positioned in particular sections of the page (or hook).

1. Let's go to **Back Office | Modules**.

2. Click on the **Positions** tab.

Here you will see a list of hooks (blocks) that you have installed and the modules within them.

Let's take an example of the right column block. You can see a list of modules, which are within the hook in the following screenshot:

Here you have the **Cart block**, the **New products block**, and the **Top seller block.** In this list, click on the up and down icons to change the module's display order. More details on this will be provided in the next section.

Time for action—Moving the blocks

The default positions of the blocks when they are first installed are shown in the following screenshot. Now, let's try moving the blocks to a different location.

We will try to do the following:

◆ Add a **NEW PRODUCTS** block to the left column and delete the **NEW PRODUCTS** block on the right column.

◆ Shift the **CART** to the top position on the right column and move the **TOP SELLERS** to the second position on the same column.

◆ Move the **NEWSLETTERS** block to the right column.

We need to perform the following steps:

1. Click on the **Positions** button. This will direct us to the **Back Office | Modules | Positions** page.

This page will show us all the modules already installed on the left, right, and center columns. It will also allow you to see which modules can be moved or set exceptions.

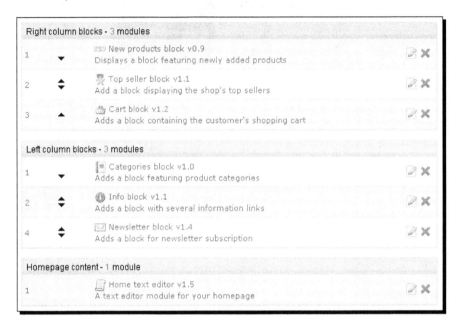

Our first task is to transplant a **NEW PRODUCTS** block on the left column.

2. Click on the **Transplant a module** button, and you will get to a page where you choose the modules you want to transplant from the drop-down list.

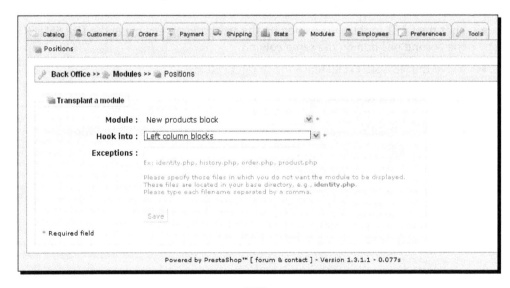

3. From the **Module** list, choose **New products block**.

4. From the **Hook into** drop-down list, you may select where you want to transplant the module into. In our case, choose the **Left column blocks.**

5. In the **Exceptions** field, type the name of the file(s) of the pages in which you do not want the module to appear. If, at this stage, you are not sure what to exclude, leave it blank; you may come back to review this setting later.

6. Click on the **Save** button. You will get a message that says **Module transplanted successfully to hook.**

It is best to install the module, hook it into the section and enter the exceptions the first time you transplant a module. If you leave it for a later stage, the changes may not be very obvious or sometimes seem ineffective. It is better to delete the module. Go to transplant and hook it again with the exceptions keyed in.

7. Preview the changes in your front office.

The next task is to delete the **NEW PRODUCTS** block from the right.

1. Go to the **Positions** tab.
2. Look up the **Right column block** list.
3. Delete the **New products block** by clicking the close icon on the right.
4. You should get the message **Module removed successfully from hook.**

Our next task is to shift the **CART** to the top position on the right column and move the **TOP SELLERS** block to the second position in the same column.

1. Go to the **Positions** tab.

2. Move the cart by dragging the **Cart block** to the top deck of the **Right column block** list when you see a four headed arrow as you move the mouse over the module you want to re-position.

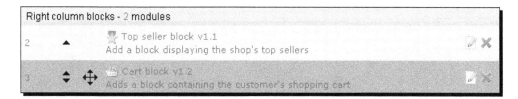

3. Once you have dragged the module to the top, it will appear above the **Top seller block** in the front office.

Our next task is to move the **NEWSLETTERS** block from the left column to the right column.

1. Go to the **Positions** tab.

2. Click on the **Transplant a module** tab.

3. Then repeat the same steps as we did when choosing the **Module** as the **Newsletter block** and **Hook into** as the **Right column blocks**

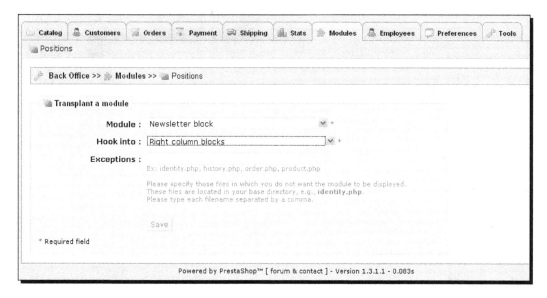

4. Click on the **Save** button.

5. Again, you should get the message that says **Module transplanted successfully to hook.**

6. You will see that the Newsletter block module is already listed within the right block.

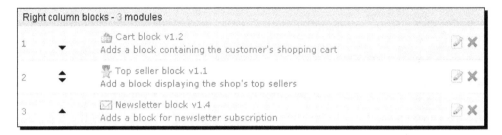

7. Now, delete the **Newsletter block** in the left column by clicking the delete button.

8. Preview your changes in the front office.

What just happened?

You performed a few fundamental tasks in building your online store. You learned how to position your modules including moving blocks within columns and moving them from one column to another.

On top of positioning the module blocks on hooks, you also learned that we can put exceptions on where the modules should appear.

If you do not want to show any particular module, for example, the **New Product blocks** in the side columns of the **order.php** page, you may insert this on the page.

You may do this with other modules in the left and right columns. After completing this stage, you will need to look at the other page elements which will be discussed in the next chapter.

Have a go hero—Configuring the module on your page

With what we have explored in the previous section, see if you can configure and edit the editorial block in the centre column. Get an image for the centre piece that is related to your store. Replace the current image with this new image.

Sometimes, the editor does not show the change that has been made, even though the front page has already shown the updated image. Always refresh your browser after you update the editor to view your front page changes when you make any adjustments.

The PrestaShop default theme image on the center is sized 530x238 pixels. You will need to adjust the size of your own image accordingly. The sample image we used is 550x394 pixels. Be careful with the width of the image as it may interfere with the three-column layout.

You may also edit the link to the image on this editorial block by modifying the **Homepage logo link** in this editor

Edit the contents of the editorial block, which appear on the front page of your site. Editing the **Introductory texts** is possible using the WYSIWYG editor. You can do almost anything here for example, insert an image, embed media (Flash, Shockwave, Real Media, Windows Media, QuickTime, and so on), indent a paragraph, change the font, and so on.

Pop Quiz

1. Where do you go in the back office to transplant the module within your PrestaShop site?

    a. **Back Office | Tools**

    b. **Back Office | Modules | Positions**

    c. **Back Office | Modules | Preferences**

2. What is a Hook?

    a. A module used in PrestaShop

    b. A block that houses the enabled modules

    c. The left column

Summary

Specifically, using the layout settings of the PrestaShop default theme, we covered how to make the following through minor adjustments from the back office without much technical knowledge being required:

◆ Installing and enabling module blocks

◆ Adding the module blocks in the columns

◆ Transplanting modules and hooking modules

◆ Moving modules within columns

◆ Updating the editorial block in the center column.

In the next chapter, we will cover how to set up the key elements in your store through configuring the module blocks including setting up the editorial block, the **Featured Products** block, and the **Catalog** function from the back office. You will also work on the other key module blocks, the top, header, footer, logo, and so on. All these complete the look of the store and will be covered when working on the back office administration. Also, we will get a sneak-peek at customizing the theme files.

3
Customizing PrestaShop Theme
Part 2

In the previous chapter, you learned about selecting, installing, and positioning the appropriate modules for your store. You also discovered how you can modify the key default modules through the back office, in order to customize your web page navigation and layouts.

We will now proceed with configuring and customizing the other key elements of your online store through the back office.

This chapter will help you set up your key elements for the PrestaShop store: The title, top of page, footer, logos, featured products. This will be a part and parcel of what you need to do. It also completes the look of the store you are designing through the back office administration. You will also begin to explore the relevant files you need to work with in customizing your own theme.

Let's move on with our next step.

Of course, exploring every tab in the back office would be advantageous, but we will specifically touch only those points that will affect your theming process. We will now look at how we can modify the following:

- Logo
- Top of page
- Adding FEATURED PRODUCTS block
- Footer

◆ Title

◆ Placing the other modules useful for your store on other section of your pages.

Before going further, I would like to emphasize two important points. They are:

1. Always work on a copy of your default theme:

    ❑ If you have not copied the default theme file, I would advise that when you start your development work, you copy the default theme file so that you have a backup or a comparison to work with.

    ❑ We will be working on the copy of the default theme, as in some cases, we will still change a few lines of codes to modify the theme. This means that if you ever make a huge blunder, you will at least have the original to start with again. If the worst ever happens, you can always upload the original file again to overwrite your errors, but that will be a big waste of time.

2. Keep a quick reference list of any modifications made to any file:

    ❑ It may sound a bit tedious, but you will find this advice useful to heed. There are a few ways of making modifications to your theme, sometimes through modification of your other files (which are not in the theme folder).

    ❑ You may copy the file and put it into the theme folder to make the changes, or it is also possible to merely modify them by overwriting the file in its location.

    ❑ Whichever way you chose, when you need to modify files which are not in your custom theme folder, you should make a quick note of what changes you have made and where have you made them.

    ❑ Why? Because when there is a new version of PrestaShop, you will need to upgrade your PrestaShop site, thus the modifications you have made will be lost. The modifications in the theme folders will remain even if you update the version of your PrestaShop site.

    ❑ By keeping a list of the modifications you've made, it will be much easier to track back to where to re-apply them after you have upgraded your PrestaShop installation.

    ❑ Never procrastinate on making this quick list because you will always find that it is a waste of time to find and trace those changes later; even just six months down the road.

Copying the default theme file

When you download PrestaShop, by default, you will have a copy of the PrestaShop theme folder.

Go to the `PrestaShop_1.3.1/themes/PrestaShop` folder. Copy this entire folder and save it on your computer. You may rename the theme accordingly, for example, `theme1`. Compress this into a `ZIP` file.

Upload the renamed folder into the `themes` directory on your hosting through your cPanel or FTP.

You will now have two themes in your `/themes` folder which are `PrestaShop` and `theme1`.

You can now log in to your PrestaShop **Back Office | Preferences | Appearance** and switch to your `theme1` that you just installed and click on the **Save** button.

On this page, you may also control what logo, favicon, and the navigation pipes you want to use throughout your website.

Now, let's start with the modification of these theme elements to complete the look of your new theme.

Logo

A logo is an important element of a company's or store's image, and it can contribute to the brand's marketing success. Therefore, getting a good quality logo is fundamental for the business.

Getting a unique and attractive logo design can be daunting, especially for those who are not born with a flair for design. However, fortunately, there are various resources that you can use to get ideas or even create a very professional looking logo that you can use in your new online store.

Some online resources for logo designs can be found at:

- ♦ `http://www.logomaker.com`—This is an online resource that allows you to freely create a logo, but you have to pay to download your new creation, which basically uses their online inputs. Quite attractive and interesting looking logos can be found and designed here.

- http://cooltext.com—This one describes itself as **A free graphics generator for web pages and anywhere else you need an impressive logo without a lot of design work**. It allows you to choose the image you would like through a few simple steps. You only need to enter the words or company name using a form and you'll have your own custom image created on the fly. The logo you designed is downloadable for free.

- http://www.simwebsol.com/ImageTool/Default.aspx—This is a Web 2.0 logo generator. Free to use and download. It requires you to fill in a few fields and generates the image file quite easily. However, the background is limited to RGB flat choices and you only have 23 images that can be chosen from to insert.

Another element, which is quite important here, is the favicon. The Favicon is the little icon representing the website you are visiting which gets displayed in the address bar of every browser.

Usually, the favicon and the logo are the same thing, except for their sizes and the formats.

They are not necessarily the same though. You may find some online resources that you can use to generate a favicon for the store. Make sure you have prepared the favicon icon before you try to replace the current favicon.

> If you are unsure of how to go about making a favicon, you may generate it online (using, http://www.favicon.cc/ or http://www.freefavicon.com/). Save the file on your hard drive and then upload it to your PrestaShop store. Uploading it is shown in the next section.

Time for action—Replacing the default logo and favicon on your site

1. The logo and the favicon can be replaced through **Back Office | Preferences | Appearance**, as shown in the following screenshot:

2. **Browse** the file you want to use from your computer.

3. Upload the files and click on the **Save** button.

4. You need to refresh your back office browser before you replace the logo and the new `favicon.ico` file.

5. You also need to clean up your browser's cache and refresh the browser to see the favicon in the frontend of the website.

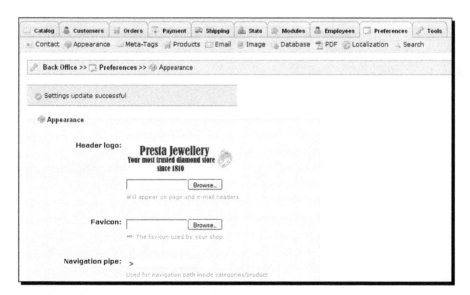

6. Upon saving and refreshing your browser, the updated images will be displayed.

What just happened?

In this simple exercise, you have just uploaded the logo that you had created, and PrestaShop has, by default, placed it in the correct directory in your new `theme1` directory through the back office panel.

> If you did not choose the new theme, for example, `theme1` in **Preferences | Appearance** under **Themes**, the logo you upload will go to the wrong directory.

The Center Editorial Block

The Center Editorial Block is where you see the main image at the center column, as we indicated previously in the front office.

This is an important block, as this is where your visitors first arrive when they visit your store. It gives a first impression to your site visitor, and therefore, you need to consider what to include in it very carefully. You will see more things that can be done here in *Chapter 7, Tips and Trick to Make PrestaShop Theme Easier* when we start using some third party modules.

Time for action—Modifying the Center Editorial Block

The Centre Editorial Block can be modified through **Back Office | Modules | Tools | Home text editor**.

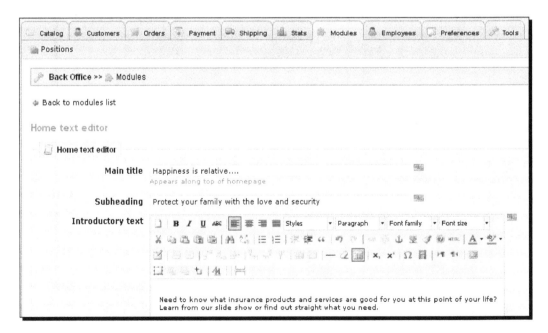

In this section, you can also edit the Centre Block image, which is referred to as **Homepage's logo**, and this title can be quite misleading as it may be confused with the actual logo. However, we have covered this matter in the previous chapter and did a mapping of each field here to the front office page of the store.

You only need to upload the image you want to replace it with and continue with editing the **Homepage logo link**, which is the link for this image (**Homepage's logo**). You may just leave it set to your current website address if you want (for example, www.mydomainname.com). You can also leave it blank if you don't want the image to be a link.

Furthermore, you will see **Homepage logo subheading**, which is the small letters you see on the default theme page that appear under the image.

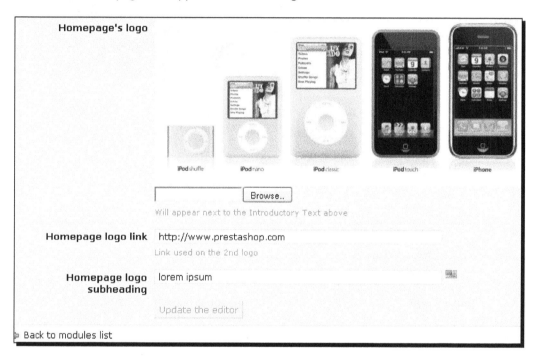

Let's replace the **Homepage's logo** image, **Homepage logo link**, and a new **Homepage logo subheading**:

1. Click on the **Update the editor** button.

2. Review your changes in your front office browser.

3. You will need to refresh the page once to see the effect.

It is possible to work with different image sizes, but the width of the image will "disturb" your column settings. If you are not going to make any unnecessary changes, then it is best to use images of the safe maximum width for the center column which is 530 pixels. If you exceed this width it will push your right column outside the standard browser view.

Now let's have a look at what you have achieved so far.

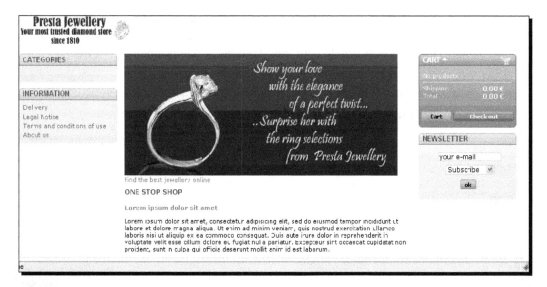

What just happened?

You have modified your Center Editorial Block by inserting a new **Homepage's logo** image, **Homepage logo link**, and a new **Homepage logo subheading**.

Top of pages block

Based on the layout structure of PrestaShop theme that we learned previously, we will look at the header section of the page. The default layout comprises the following in the header section:

1. **Currency** block (links to the available currencies used on the site).

2. **Languages** block (links to the available language translation of the pages interface).

3. **Permanent link** block:

   ❏ **Contact** (icon that links to the contact form page)

   ❏ **Sitemap** (icon that links to the sitemap page)

   ❏ **Bookmark** (icon that helps you bookmark a particular page on the site)

4. **Search** block

5. User links block:

   ❑ **Your Account** (icon that links to the login page or registration page). When logged in, it links to the account page that lists everything the customer can do with their account. It is only when the viewer is logged out that it links to the authentication page

   ❑ **Cart** (icon that links to the shopping cart summary page)

   ❑ **Welcome**, **Log in** (links to the login page or registration page)

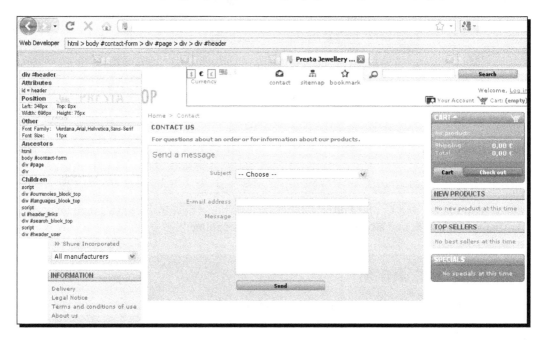

Time for action—Modifying the Top of pages

To get these elements back on the pages, you will need to install and enable the relevant modules. These simple steps will need little modifications unless you want to add a new currency and a new language.

Let's enable these modules through these simple steps:

1. **Currency block**—go to **Modules** | scroll down to **Blocks** | **Currency block**.

2. **Languages block**—go to **Modules** | scroll down to **Blocks** | **Language block**.

3. **Search block**—go to **Modules** | scroll down to **Blocks** | **Quick Search block**.

4. **Permanent link block**—go to **Modules** | scroll down to **Blocks** | **Permanent links block**.

By default, these modules tend to appear on the pages in the order you installed and enabled them. The first one will appear the leftmost while the last one will be the rightmost. You can shift the arrangement by installing them according to what you want to appear on the leftmost or the rightmost sides. Notice that the **Permanent link** block is on the right as we enabled it last. There is an easier way to do this as well, which we will cover in the next section.

You can modify this by working on the position of the modules within the **Top of pages** hooks.

 There are two similar hooks, which can be quite confusing, that is, the **Top of pages** and **Header**. The blocks are positioned or "transplanted" in a **Top of pages** hook and not **Header of pages**.

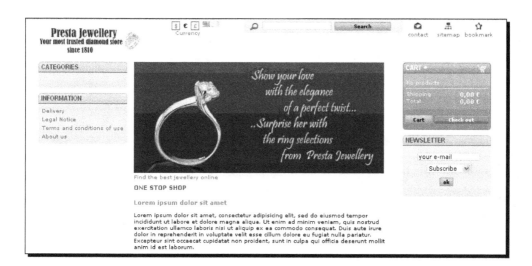

The **Welcome**, **Log in**, **Cart**, and the User login links can be enabled through **Back Office | Modules | Blocks | User info block**. Upon installing and enabling the module, you will have the **Welcome**, **Log in**, **Your Account**, and **Cart** link displayed on your front office. By default, all those are automatically hooked to the **Top of pages** once they are enabled. If it is not, you can have it hooked through transplanting the module to the hook, as shown in the next screenshot. This can be done by following these simple steps:

1. Go to **Back Office | Modules | Position | Transplant a module**.

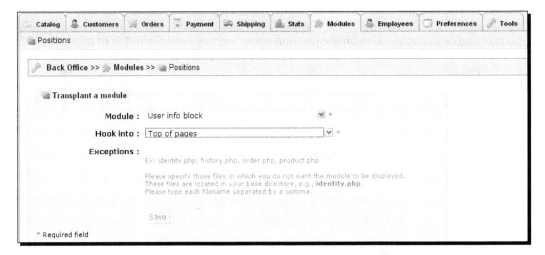

2. Choose the **Module** you want to transplant from the drop-down menu.

3. Choose the hook from **Hook into**, the one you want the **Module** to go into.

4. Click on the **Save** button.

The arrangement of the blocks can be done by moving them around within the hooks, which we will see next.

Go to **Modules | Positions**. There you can arrange the position of the modules within the hooks by dragging each of them to the required position as we have learned in the previous chapter. As you can see, there are the two similar hooks which may be confusing, namely, the **Header of pages** and the **Top of pages**.

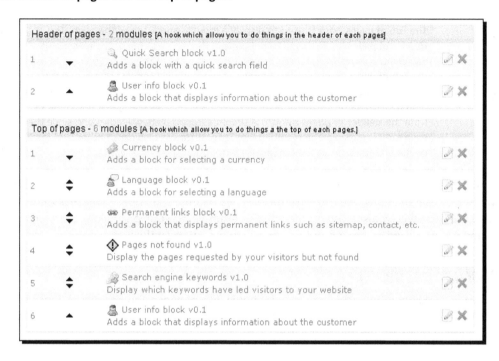

Compare it with what you have at the front office in the next screenshot.

The **Quick Search block** does not appear despite it being hooked at the **Header of pages**. The other blocks which are hooked to the **Top of pages** are displayed in the front office. The same thing with the **User info block**; you only see the one which is hooked to the **Top of pages** and not the one in the **Header of pages**.

> The **Top of pages** hook is used to display a module at the top of the page. The **Header of pages** hook is used to put code in the `<head>` tag of the website. If you want to move a module or delete it from the top of the page, you should use the **Top of pages** hook, not the **Header of pages** hook. Modules that are in the **Header of pages** hook should not be removed, since they are required for the module to function correctly. For example, if you remove the **Quick search block** from the **Header of pages** hook, the search autocomplete will not work, since the code for it is missing. The resulting JavaScript error will also cause other problems on the website such as the **Categories block** not displaying any categories.

To move the modules to the left or right, you need to move them up within the hook. The lower it is within the hook, the more to the right the module will appear, whereas the upper within the hook will be displayed on the left. For example, the **Currency** block is first in the list, and it is displayed on the left of the **Top of pages** section on the webpage.

What just happened?

You just learned the differences between the hooks **Top of pages** and **Header of pages** in PrestaShop. You also get to modify the blocks you want to use on the top of the page and how to move them around within the hook.

The FEATURED PRODUCTS block

The **FEATURED PRODUCTS** block is the one below the Center Editorial block.

This block can be enabled through **Modules | Tools | Featured Products on the Homepage v0.9.**

The default number of featured products is ten. You can add more if you have a lot of items to feature by changing this amount.

What you want to do now is to add the products (and their images) to this featured block.

The location of the images file would be in the image folder /
PrestaShop/img/p/…….jpg

When you upload the image files on the product page, it will be saved into the particular folder which is not in the theme folder. Therefore, if you change to another theme, the product images will remain.

To ensure that a product is displayed on the **FEATURED PRODUCTS** block, it is imperative to have it appear on the home and on the particular category.

Time for action—Adding the FEATURED PRODUCTS block

The function of the **FEATURED PRODUCTS** block is to highlight certain products on your home page. We will now install the **FEATURED PRODUCTS** block:

1. Go to **Back Office | Modules | Featured Products** in the home page module.

2. After you installed and enabled the **FEATURED PRODUCTS** block, you will need to configure it.

3. When you click on >>**Configure**, you will be directed to the following page:

The default number of featured products that will be displayed in the **FEATURED PRODUCTS** block in your front office is **four**, but as previously mentioned, in the back office it is stated that the default number of featured products allowed is **10**. This setting can be modified at any time, should you ever decide that you want to change the number of featured products.

What just happened?

You have just enabled the **FEATURED PRODUCTS** block.

Time for action—Adding an item as a Featured Product

To add **FEATURED PRODUCTS** to your front office home page, perform the following steps:

1. Go to **Back Office** | **Catalog** | **Categories** | and scroll down to **Products in this Category**.

2. If you are using the default theme, you will see a list of product items that you can edit.

3. Click on the pencil icon next to one of them (the edit icon on the right).

4. You will be directed to the particular product page. Here, you will see a number of tabs within the page. The next screenshot illustrates what you will see in the back office:

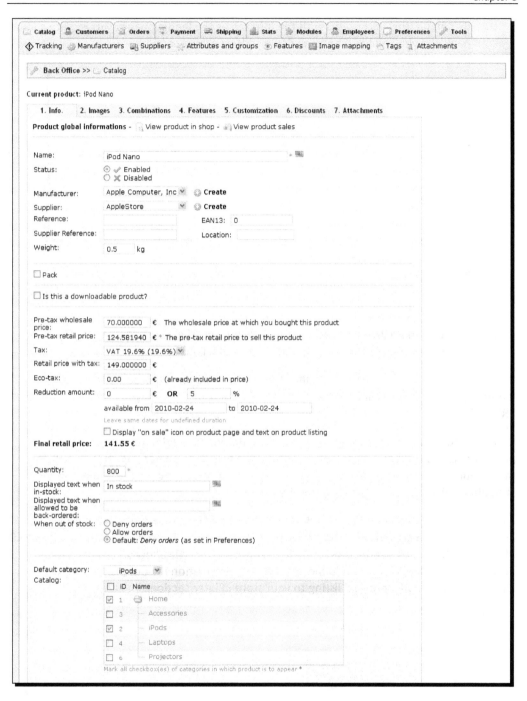

5. By default, this part opens with the **Info** tab as the landing page. This is quite a long page and you will need to scroll down to the **Catalog** section.

6. In the **Catalog** section, mark the **Home** checkbox, as shown in the preceding screenshot. Here you can also enable the box setting where the new item should be categorized.

7. Scroll down further, and click on the **Save** button. The item will now display in the **FEATURED PRODUCTS** section of your front office home page.

It is not necessary to change the default category to **Home** for the product to appear as a featured product. By enabling **Home**, it is sufficient for it to be displayed in the **FEATURED PRODUCTS** block.

It is better to make another category (apart from **Home**) as the default category for the product because the default category is used in the breadcrumb bar and friendly URL for the product. If you disable **Home**, it will only appear on the product page and not in the **FEATURED PRODUCTS** block (that is, on the home page)

As mentioned previously, in the default theme, there will be a maximum of ten items displayed in the **FEATURED PRODUCTS** block at any one time. In order to increase **FEATURED PRODUCTS** items, you need to configure it accordingly. This will allow you to have more products, and you will have to add more items and information in your product listing. We will cover how to add a product listing to your store in later sections.

To remove a product currently displayed on your online store home page, you need to disable the box next to **Home** in the **Catalog** section of the particular product's admin product page.

When you add an item to display on the **FEATURED PRODUCTS** block, by default, the last item will appear to the right of the block. If you want to re-arrange the position of the product featured, you can perform the following steps:

1. Go to the **Back Office** | **Catalog** | and scroll down to **Products in this Category**.

2. Go to the **Position** column and when you move your cursor on it, the four arrow will appear, drag the product that you want to sort to the position you prefer.

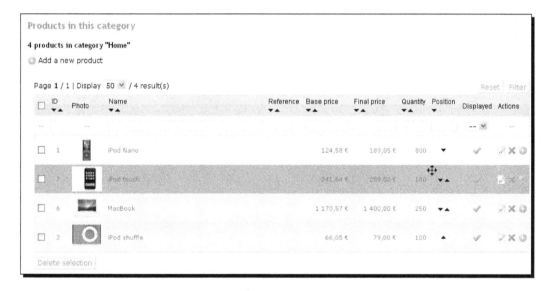

What just happened?

You just learned how to add the products to the **FEATURED PRODUCTS** block on the home page.

Time for action—To edit, display, or delete a Featured Product

At some point you might change your mind and want to edit the information of your **FEATURED PRODUCTS** block; you can do a few things such as editing, deleting, and turning on and off the display. Editing and deleting is pretty straightforward - you just need to click on the edit icon and the delete icon respectively.

You can display the product or turn it off by clicking on the button on the right under the **Displayed** column. If you turn off, a product it will not be displayed in the **FEATURED PRODUCTS** box. It will appear in **Category** or **Manufacturer** listing when someone clicks on, say, **Laptops** (if it is listed under **Laptops** category) or the manufacturer's name.

Time for action—Adding a new product to your FEATURED PRODUCTS block

There are a few key things you may want to set prior to adding new products to your **FEATURED PRODUCTS** block:

♦ Information on the manufacturer (optional, but necessary if you use the **Manufacturers** module in your store)

♦ An image for the product

Now let's perform the following steps:

1. Go back to **Back Office | Catalog |** and scroll down to **Product in this Category**.

2. Click on the **Add a new product** button. It will open a new page, which has two tabs (**Info** and **Images**), as shown in the following screenshot:

3. Fill the necessary fields. Go to the **Default Category** enable the box next to **Home**. This was similar to the process when we wanted to include the products into the **FEATURED PRODUCTS** block section.

The **FEATURED PRODUCTS** block will show all the images that are at its maximum value in its configuration.

For this example, let us assume that you have six products which are set to be featured at the **FEATURED PRODUCTS** block. And, you had configured the **FEATURED PRODUCTS** block to display eight items. It is best that you match the number of items in the row (in this case four items per row), so that it does not look incomplete as there will be blank spaces in the block as shown in the following screenshot:

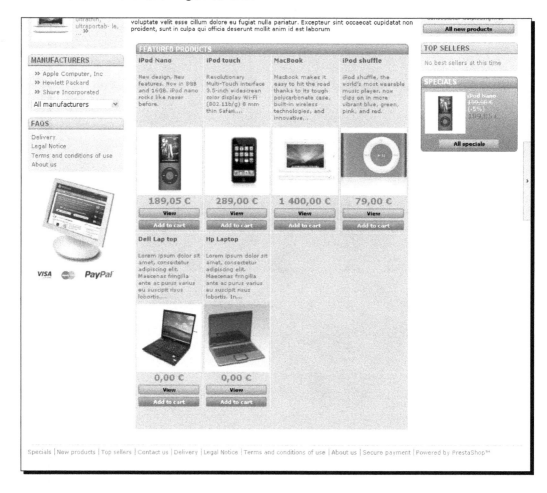

What just happened?

You learned how to add more new products to the Featured Product block.

Footer

Now we will work on the footer block. Go to the **Back Office | Modules | Blocks | Footer links block**. You will notice in your front office that a few links are enabled by default. They are the **Specials**, **New Products**, **Top Sellers**, **Contact Us**, and **Powered by PrestaShop**. These will be covered later in this chapter.

The links shown in the following screenshot are controlled by configuring the footer module through the back office. The checked items are those added to the default footer links and they will be shown on your front office browser. To display the rest, just tick the check box on the left.

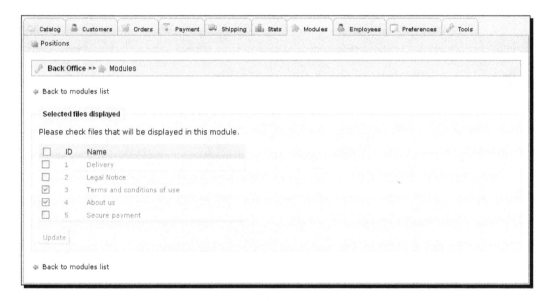

So, how do you add a new link, which is not in the configure list, of the footer?

Time for action—Adding new pages on the Footer Link block

Let's add a new page to your footer.

1. Say you want to have a page on privacy policy, which you will call **Privacy.**

2. Go to **Tools | CMS**, and click on the **Add new** button.

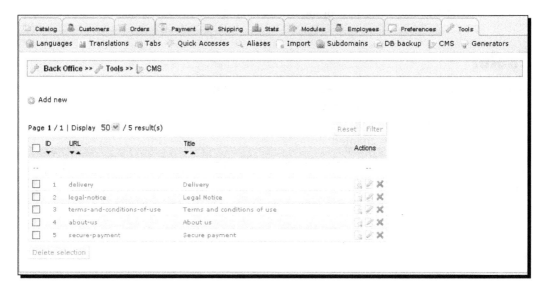

3. You will then be directed to a new page where you can create a new content page.

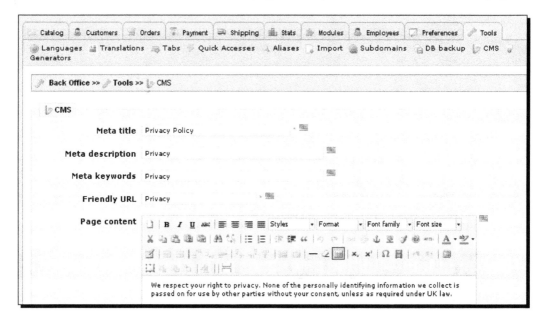

4. Fill out the information, and click on the **Save** button.

5. You will see this new page on the list once the creation is successful. However, this page is not linked to any blocks yet. If you want this page to be linked to in the footer, you will need to enable it in the **Footer Link** module.

6. Go back to **Back Office | Modules | Blocks | Footer links block**, enable the boxes, click on **>>Configure** and check the box next to the Privacy Policy and then click on the **Update** button.

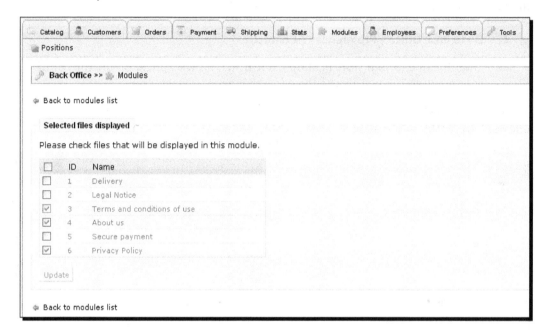

7. You will be able to see it on your footer link at the front office.

What just happened?

We just added a new link to the footer block.

Title

The title is what you see on top of the browser. It is an important part of your website, especially if you want your website to be found easily through search engines. Therefore, you must consider what should appear there carefully.

Time for action—Modifying your page title

In order to modify your page's title:

1. Go to **Back Office | Preferences | Contact**.

2. Enter the title to your store in **Shop name** field. This will appear on the top bar of your browser. This will also be the name that appears in your e-mails.

This choice of title is an important part of search engine optimization and some search engines look for this information when they rank your pages.

This is how it appears on the front office.

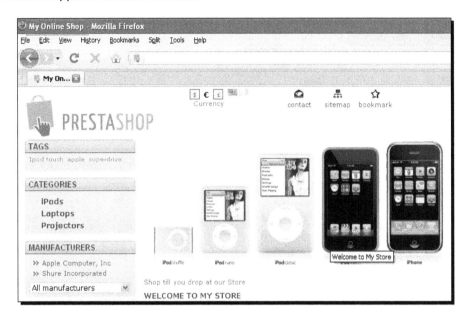

If you want to change the title for this **index.php** page within your store, you will need to make adjustments to the **Meta-Tags** as follows:

1. Go to **Back Office** | **Preferences** | **Meta-Tags**.

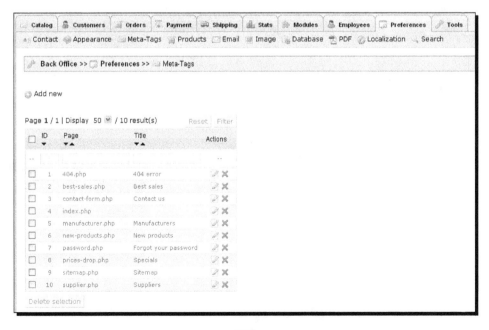

2. Choose the page **index.php**, and click on the edit icon on the right (the pencil icon).

3. Enter the **Page's title**. In this example, we have entered in **Shop till you Drop!**. Then click on the **Save** button.

The next screenshot shows what happens in the frontend.

By default, for the products page, the page title will show the main page title and the product name.

The shop name and product name is displayed in the title bar if a meta title isn't specified. The meta title changes the title bar only, not the product name or heading, which is always the product name.

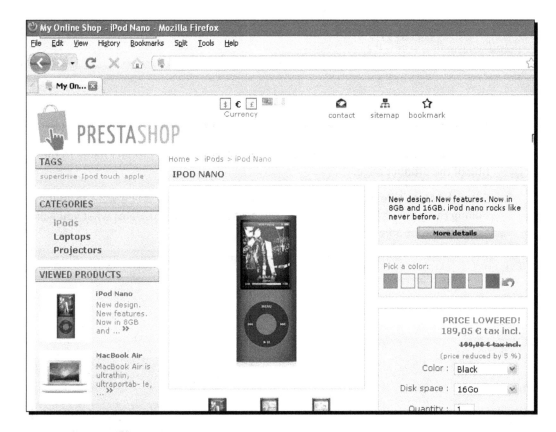

If you want to change the page title to something else, you will have to edit the **meta title** of the product page. You can change the title of the products by performing these simple steps:

1. Go to the **Back Office | Catalog |** and scroll down to the **Products in this Category**.

2. Choose a product, and click on the pencil icon.

3. Click on **Click here to improve product's rank in search engines (SEO)** to change the **Meta title**.

Let's assume that you want to add something other than the product name to the title of the product page.

4. Enter the **Meta title**, and click on the **Save** (or **Save and Stay**, if you want to continue editing this page after saving) button. The next screenshot illustrates what you will see in the front office:

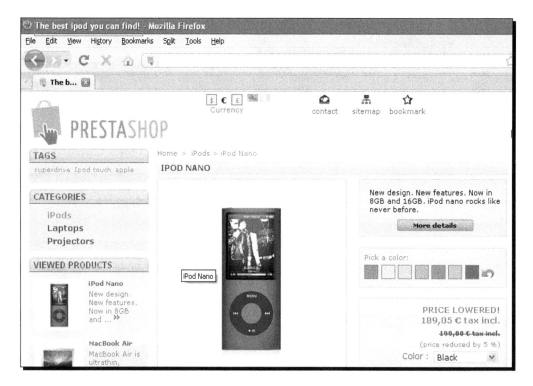

What just happened?

You modified the page title of the main page and the product page.

Modules block

Now that you are getting familiar with the **modules** tab, you may be interested to know how to modify the modules name or what appears on the front office in the module block. For example, you may want to change the name of the **INFORMATION** block to **FAQS**.

Time for action—Modifying block names

1. Go to **Back Office | Tools | Translations.**

2. In the **Modify translations** section, all parts of the translation are listed in a drop-down menu. You need to select **Modules translations**.

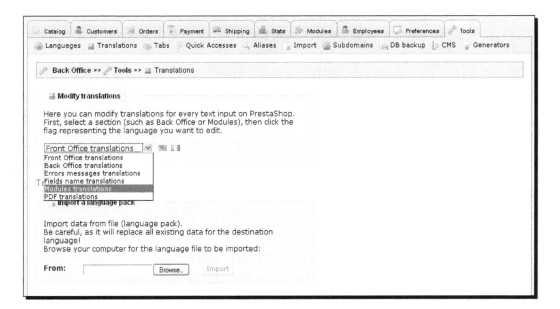

3. Next, click on the particular language flag icon. For example, click on the American flag for English. You will have to browse through the listing for the expressions you want to change. Imagine that you are looking to change the **INFORMATION** block to **FAQS**, which initially looks like the following screenshot:

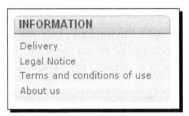

4. Go to **prestashop-blockinfos-9 expressions**. Enter the word you want to replace; in this case, **Information** is replaced by **FAQs**.

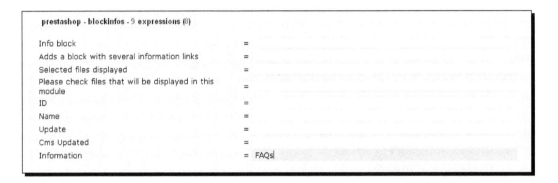

5. Finally, click on the **Update translations** button.

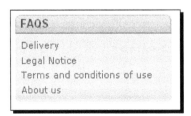

What just happened?

Here we learned how to change the name of a block. In the previous exercise, you modified a block name from **INFORMATION** to **FAQS**.

Have a go hero—Removing the "Powered by PrestaShop" at the footer link

We have not really started looking into the PrestaShop files. Nevertheless, this is a minor edit that you can easily perform without much technical knowledge.

You may need to remove the **Powered by PrestaShop** located at the footer link. Removal of this link is often requested by clients.

You will need an editor (such as Notepad or Dreamweaver) to open and edit the correct file to remove the **Powered by PrestaShop** line, as you cannot do it through the back office panel.

There are two ways of "removing" the **Powered by PrestaShop line**.

The first method involves editing or removing the line. This can be done by looking up and removing the relevant lines within the `blockvariouslinks.tpl` file.

The file is located at: `/modules/blockvariouslinks/blockvariouslinks.tpl`.

Copy this particular file to your themes folder. You should have this kind of link to the `blockvariouslinks.tpl` after you have copied it to the theme file (in this case, the theme folder name is `theme1`; you have to find it in your own theme folder).

For the `theme1` that I have, the file path should look something like this:

`/themes/theme1/modules/blockvariouslinks/blockvariouslinks.tpl`

You will have to look up your own theme file accordingly.

Look for this code in the `blockvariouslink.tpl` file:

```
<li class="last_item">{l s='Powered by' mod='blockvariouslinks'}
<a href="http://www.PrestaShop.com">PrestaShop</a>&trade;</li>
```

After removing it, save the file.

Another method of "removing" the link involves not deleting the lines but commenting them. This is common for those familiar with the HTML method of commenting on files. This is particularly useful when you need to look back at your files later as you will find it much faster to decipher the code in your pages.

To comment out lines in HTML, you can insert the starting comment tag, which is `<!--` (that's the 'lesser than' sign followed by an exclamation mark and two dashes) and the ending tag, which is `-->`. The browser does not display any text placed between these tags.

However, a better solution in PrestaShop is to use the Smarty comment tags {* and *} instead of the HTML tags <!-- and -->. By using Smarty comments, the code is ignored when the HTML is generated.

When you use <!-- and -->, the code is still visible when you view the source of the website and is unnecessarily downloaded.

Although it is allowed by PrestaShop to delete the whole line, commenting it out is a good choice, both as a reference for future editors and as a way to maintain the information intact in acknowledging the developers' effort in their free contributions to your final work.

In the end, the line would look like this.

```
{*
<li class="last_
item">{l s='Powered by' mod='blockvariouslinks'} <a href="http://www.
PrestaShop.com">PrestaShop</a>&trade;</li>
*}
```

You can also modify or delete the code we mentioned and instead replace it inserting <!--Powered By PrestaShop--> or {*Powered by PrestaShop*}

Summary

We have covered the following modifications of the default theme through back office:

- ◆ Modifying the logo
- ◆ Modifying the Center Editorial block
- ◆ Modifying the header
- ◆ Modifying the Featured Product
- ◆ Adding a new item to the Featured Products block
- ◆ Modifying the footer
- ◆ Modifying the titles
- ◆ Changing a block's name
- ◆ Removing "Powered By" by editing the code

In the next chapter, we will explore ways to edit more code in the PrestaShop files in order to develop our new themes.

4

Adjusting Style Sheets

In this chapter, you will learn about **Cascading Style Sheet** *(CSS) and how they are used in a PrestaShop theme. You will also learn about modifying the background colors of blocks and web pages, text fonts, text sizes, and the text colors. We will then cover how to modify block borders and their colors. We will also cover how to modify the paragraph. All through simple modifications to the CSS file.*

To start with, if you simply follow the steps given in here, it is enough for you to modify the CSS files in PrestaShop. However, it is useful to learn about CSS to be able to apply the knowledge to other sections (pages) of your PrestaShop site, if required.

To be more precise, you will learn the following in this chapter:

- ◆ A little bit about Cascading Style Sheets
- ◆ The CSS files in PrestaShop
- ◆ Modifying the fonts, the text colors, and the text sizes
- ◆ Changing the background colors
- ◆ Modifying the border color of blocks
- ◆ Modifying the paragraph in the center column

Getting to know the basics of PrestaShop theme

Before we get to know the basics of the PrestaShop theme CSS file, we need to get to know the tool we will be using to modify and check our files.

At this stage, you would have used Firefox at least for browsing websites. It is useful to go deeper than using it for browsing, as Firefox comes with many web development tools that can be very handy for working on your websites.

Other than those Notepads or editors we mentioned in the previous chapter, we will have to download and get hold of a web developer's tool which can be either Firebug or Web Developer extension.

Firebug can be downloaded from: `www.getfirebug.com`

Click on **Install Firebug For Firefox**. Alternatively, you can also download it from Mozilla's Firefox Add-ons site.

Install it, restart Firefox, and it is ready to use.

Another common tool for web development is the Web Developer tool, which can be used with Firefox and Google Chrome. It is also an excellent tool that can assist you in your theming work.

The Web Developer extension can be downloaded from: `http://chrispederick.com/work/web-developer/`

Try saving the extension to your machine (by right-clicking or ctrl-clicking the download link and choosing **Save Link As...**) and dragging the saved extension into your browser window to start the installation.

You can use them both together or separately. Note that any changes you made through the Web Developer tool or Firebug are only good for reviewing and editing them to see the effect of your action. To make it work for your theme, you will have to apply the changes to your `global.css` file and save it. This can be done through an online editor through your cPanel or via FTP. If you are not sure how to go about this, the process is elaborated in *Chapter 6, Steps for Creating Themes*.

We will now look into the PrestaShop default theme, which is packed as standard theme in PrestaShop.

Time for action—Getting to know the PrestaShop CSS files

1. Open your PrestaShop directory either on your computer or the web server.

2. Next, navigate to the default `themes` folder (`prestashop_1.3/themes/prestashop`) or you can look at your new theme folder.

3. Now, let's get a better look at each of the important files within it that we will work with.

> In the previous chapter, you learned about copying this default PrestaShop theme file to build another new theme.

4. Go to your FTP or cPanel administration and look up the new theme folder you have just created (for example, `../themes/theme1/`).

5. Locate the CSS folder.

6. The next screenshot shows where to locate the `/css` folder:

Within this CSS folder, you will see three CSS files:

1. `global.css`
2. `maintenance.css`
3. `scenes.css`

These CSS files work with the Smarty template files (`.tpl`), which are, by default, located in the `modules` directory. We have not really got to know "Smarty" that much yet, but we will begin to do some work here on the Smarty template files. For now, we will show you the steps to change your CSS file and understand the relationship with the relevant template (`.tpl`) files. We will elaborate more on "Smarty" in *Chapter 6, Steps for Creating Themes*.

The `global.css` file can be daunting for a beginner as it has many lines. It can make it difficult for you to find the right lines to edit in order to modify your web page's appearance.

Instead of dissecting the entire file, our tasks will be based on the required output, which will be a result of the modifications we make to the elements.

There will be times when we will refer to certain lines, and you may not see the same thing in your CSS file, as this is depending on the web developer tools you use. This is more likely to happen when you copy another theme file which may have been modified. Here we have used both Web Developer tools and Firebug on Firefox alternately or both. The key point is to look up the sections as indicated in the CSS file through /* */.

A brief background to Cascading Style Sheets

Let's get acquainted with what actually controls the color, font, and the formatting of your web pages. For this chapter, we will start with simple editing of the existing CSS files.

We won't be giving you a full course on CSS, as these theme modifications can easily be done through altering the syntaxes as we will show you how without even really understanding it. For starters, if you already know CSS, this chapter may be too easy for you. If we stick with explaining CSS too much in detail, this chapter will be very dry and we may as well start a book on CSS! You should find the following sections very interesting, as you will be seeing the changes of your modification in an instance.

As a background, CSS controls the structure and the look/appearance of your web pages. It separates the structure and design elements from the content of a web page. CSS is the design instructions that are linked to HTML/XHTML documents, which in the past were done quite painfully through repetitive design markups.

The syntax of CSS is easy to understand. If you do not have much knowledge about the syntax, the following are the basic necessities required for editing the CSS file.

 Those who lack knowledge of HTML and CSS and would like to learn more should visit an authoritative sites with good explanations on the topic such as: www.w3.org or www.w3schools.com.

CSS syntax

Even though we will get on with changing the syntaxes without necessarily understanding CSS through this step-by-step guide, it is imperative to at least understand a bit of CSS syntax as you will be seeing a lot of it later and can perhaps use it for other sections you want to change.

The CSS syntax basically has two main parts—a selector, and one or more declarations. This is how it looks.

```
h1 {color: white; font-size:11px; }
```

In the preceding CSS code, `h1` is the selector and also the element we control the style with, `color` and `font-size` are properties and `white` and `11px` are values.

A declaration comprises a property and a value. Declarations are separated within the brackets using semicolons. The entire line from { to } has two declarations.

The previous syntax comprises two declarations which are:

- ◆ `h1 { color: white;}`
- ◆ `h1 { font-size:11px;}`

In the next few sections, we will be changing or modifying the properties in a number of declarations.

 For more information about CSS Reference, refer to
http://www.w3schools.com/css/css_reference.asp

Prior to that, let's start with getting to know the functions of these CSS files as there are a lot of things you can do to your web pages by editing these files.

Now let's have a closer look at the Cascading Style Sheets in PrestaShop that we will be using a lot.

global.css

`global.css` is the file that controls the overall look of your site. Succinctly named global, it controls the appearance of almost every other page in your PrestaShop site.

This file controls:

- ◆ Background color
- ◆ Font size

- Font family
- Color
- Text alignment
- Paragraph format and pagination

There are a number of alternate ways to achieve a particular result in CSS. However, we will work mostly on the simple ways of editing where you only need to look up the existing syntax in the relevant sections of this `global.css` file and change the values of the properties you need to modify the elements on your web page.

Wherever applicable, we will also show you the way to insert properties and values on certain ID classes and selectors to get the same result. We will delve more into this CSS file later.

maintenance.css

During maintenance mode, if you are using the default theme, your site visitor will see the following on their browser.

The file that controls the look of the maintenance page is `maintenance.css`, which also controls the styles and structure of whatever content you have in the `maintenance.tpl` file.

This is the content of the `maintenance.css` file:

```
*, body{margin:0;padding:0}
body
{
   font-family:90%/1em 'Lucida Grande', Verdana, sans-serif
}
#maintenance
{
   width:450px;
   margin:35px auto 0 auto;
   padding:12px 0;
```

```
    background:#fff;
    text-align:center;
    text-transform:none;
    font-weight:normal;
    letter-spacing:0;
    color: #C73178
}
#message
{
    width:450px;
    margin-top:35px;
    padding:12px 15px;
    border-top:1px dotted #666;
    border-bottom:1px dotted #666;
    background:#F9E3EE;
    text-align:justify;
    font:90%/1em 'Lucida Grande', Verdana, sans-serif;
    text-transform:none;
    font-weight:normal;
    letter-spacing:0;
    color:#C73178
}
#message img
{
    padding:30px
}
```

There are three main ID selectors in this CSS file. The `maintenance`, `message`, and
`message img` (those with the #). The following image is the default maintenance mode
page with selectors labeled accordingly:

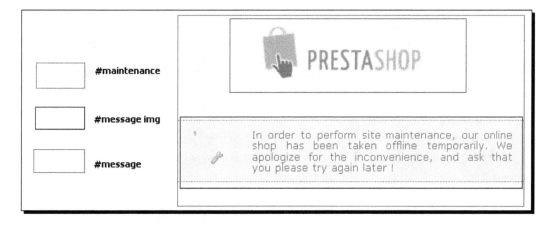

The preceding image shows how the ID selectors are related to how site visitors see those elements in the front office.

The following is the `maintenance.tpl` file that the `maintenance.css` controls:

```
<!DOCTYPE html PUBLIC "-//W3C//DTD XHTML 1.0 Transitional//EN"
"http://www.w3.org/TR/xhtml1/DTD/xhtml1-transitional.dtd">
<html xmlns="http://www.w3.org/1999/xhtml" xml:lang="{$lang_iso}"
lang="{$lang_iso}">
  <head>
    <title>{$meta_title|escape:'htmlall':'UTF-8'}</title>
    <meta http-equiv="Content-Type" content="text/html; charset=utf-
    8" />
{if isset($meta_description)}
    <meta name="description"
    content="{$meta_description|escape:'htmlall':'UTF-8'}" />
{/if}
{if isset($meta_keywords)}
    <meta name="keywords"
    content="{$meta_keywords|escape:'htmlall':'UTF-8'}" />
{/if}
    <meta name="robots" content="{if
    isset($nobots)}no{/if}index,follow" />
      <link rel="shortcut icon" href="{$img_dir}favicon.ico" />
      <link href="{$css_dir}maintenance.css" rel="stylesheet"
      type="text/css" />
  </head>
  <body>
    <div id="maintenance">
      <p><img src="{$content_dir}img/logo.jpg" alt="logo" /><br /><br
      /></p>
      <p id="message">
        <img src="{$content_dir}img/admin/tab-tools.gif"
        style="margin-right:10px; float:left;" alt="" />{l s='In
        order to perform site maintenance, our online shop has been
        taken offline temporarily. We apologize for the
        inconvenience, and ask that you please try again later !'}
      </p>
      <span style="clear:both;"> </span>
    </div>
  </body>
</html>
```

Time for action—Modifying the maintenance mode

Imagine that you want to change the maintenance mode screen to something else, you will need to do a few things:

1. You can change the image that is used as the logo through the back office, as we have seen in *Chapter 2, Customizing PrestaShop Theme Part I*. The same logo that you uploaded earlier will be used throughout in your e-mail and maintenance mode.

   Alternatively, we can do it by editing the code and uploading the new image to the right folder; the steps will be covered later in this chapter.

2. We have to change the following lines in your `maintenance.tpl` file and edit them according to your requirements.

   Look it up in your theme folder: `/public_html/prestashop/themes/theme1`.

   ```
   <p id="message">
     <img src="{$content_dir}img/admin/tab-tools.gif" style="margin-
     right:10px; float:left;" alt="" />{l s='In order to perform site
     maintenance, our online shop has been taken offline temporarily.
     We apologize for the inconvenience, and ask that you please try
     again later !'}
   </p>
   ```

3. Let's change it to:

   ```
   <p id="message">
     <img src="{$content_dir}img/admin/tab-tools.gif" style="margin-
     right:10px; float:left;" alt="" />{l s='This site is under
     maintenance. Please contact the following
     ABC Store Online Limited
     33 W. 111 Street, New York, NY 10001,
     USA
     Phone: (212) 210-2100 '}
   </p>
   ```

4. We have to change the color and the layout in order to play around with the CSS codes.

5. Let's change the selectors by widening the box for `#maintenance` and `#message` in the `maintenance.css` file:

```
#maintenance
{
  width:450px;
  margin:35px auto 0 auto;
  padding:12px 0;
  background:#fff;
  text-align:center;
  text-transform:none;
  font-weight:normal;
  letter-spacing:0;
  color: #C73178
}
```

6. Change it to:

```
#maintenance
{
  width:750px;
  margin:35px auto 0 auto;
  padding:12px 0;
  background:#fefefe;
  text-align:center;
  text-transform:none;
  font-weight:bold;
  letter-spacing:0;
  color: #3FCA66
}
```

7. Look for the following lines:

```
#message
{
  width:450px;
  margin-top:35px;
  padding:12px 15px;
  border-top:1px dotted #666;
  border-bottom:1px dotted #666;
  background:#F9E3EE;
  text-align:justify;
  font:90%/1em 'Lucida Grande', Verdana, sans-serif;
  text-transform:none;
  font-weight:normal;
  letter-spacing:0;
  color:#C73178
}
```

8. Change them to:

```
#message
{
  width:450px;
  margin-top:35px;
  padding:12px 15px;
  border-top:1px dotted #666;
  border-bottom:1px dotted #666;
  background:#2EE6F3;
  text-align:justify;
  font:90%/1em 'Lucida Grande', Verdana, sans-serif;
  text-transform:none;
  font-weight:normal;
  letter-spacing:0;
  color:#000
}
```

9. The maintenance icon can be replaced by uploading a new icon at `/img/admin/tab-tools.gif`

As you widened the message box, you will have to change the padding of the icon so that it is not positioned wrongly. Change the value from `30px` to `10px`.

This is dependent on the changes you make to your CSS file.

```
#message img
{
  padding:10px
}
```

Now, let us preview what you have done to the maintenance mode page.

WEBSITENAME.COM
company slogan / tagline here

This site is under maintenance. Please contact the following ABC Store Online Limited 33 W. 111 Street, New York, NY 10001, USA Phone: (212) 210-2100

What just happened?

You just modified the maintenance mode page of your PrestaShop site according to your requirements. You can do more than this by editing the entire `.tpl` file and applying more styles to it as well.

scenes.css

`scenes.css` is the file that controls your `scenes.tpl` file which manages how the pages appear on your site depending on the `js` files linked to it.

New or modified images must be placed in the new theme's image folder (for example, `../themes/theme1/img`). You normally do not need to modify this file unless you are making a drastic change.

PrestaShop uses CSS and makes use of the CSS's inheritance and cascading nature. By importing a style sheet, we can import all the style sheets that are imported by that particular style sheet. Through this method, we are creating a cascade of style sheets.

When a style sheet, which is a parent to another style sheet within the cascade, is altered, these modifications will automatically "cascade" into the web pages that are linked to the lower (child) style sheets too.

> Read more about cascading and inheritance in CSS at:
> `http://www.w3.org/TR/CSS2/cascade.html#inheritance`
> and `http://www.westciv.com/style_master/academy/css_tutorial/advanced/cascade_inheritance.html`

You can work on the CSS file by editing the `global.css` file within `theme1` (the new theme directory we created) as you already have a back up of the `global.css` file in the default PrestaShop theme.

Now, let's move on to something more interesting—changing the look of your new PrestaShop store.

Modifying colors in your theme

We will start with the fun part by adjusting the color.

It is fine to play trial and error, but there is a huge collection of information you can get from the internet on how to get the best match for your site. The best design can be produced through getting the appropriate color schemes to enhance the overall design of the output.

One of the best resources for color scheme is:
`http://colorschemedesigner.com/`
Here you can choose a color scheme for your site, and test it on a sample page that is automatically generated based on your chosen colors. You can also export the code of these color schemes to HTML and CSS.

We need to decide the background color, text, link color, border color, and so on.

So, before we dive into the style sheet, let's learn about choosing a color scheme.

Time for action—Deciding on a color scheme

Let's try choosing a color scheme for your site. You can choose the scheme using the online color schemer:

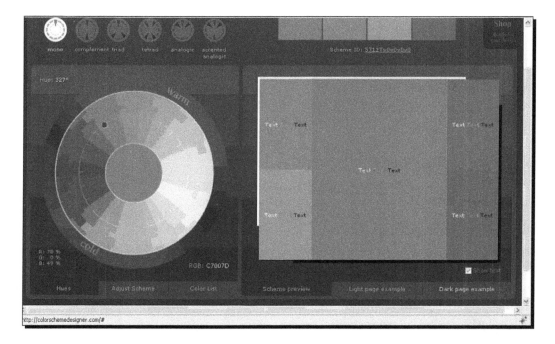

At this stage, make a note of the code of the colors used in the scheme you are building.

```
<!--
  Color Palette by Color Scheme Designer
-->
<palette>
<url>http://colorschemedesigner.com/#5011Tw0w0w0w0</url>
<colorset id="primary" title="Primary Color">
<color id="primary-1" nr="1" rgb="B70094" r="183" g="0" b="148"/>
<color id="primary-2" nr="2" rgb="892276" r="137" g="34" b="118"/>
<color id="primary-3" nr="3" rgb="770060" r="119" g="0" b="96"/>
<color id="primary-4" nr="4" rgb="DB37BC" r="219" g="55" b="188"/>
<color id="primary-5" nr="5" rgb="DB63C4" r="219" g="99" b="196"/>
</colorset>
</palette>
<!--
 Generated by Color Scheme Designer © Petr Stanicek 2002-2009
-->
```

Try using the color schemer to generate the relevant color code that have to be applied to your themes. Here, you get an idea of, say, how a background color is used with different text colors. The steps on working with this color schemer is also elaborated in *Chapter 6, Steps for Creating Themes*.

What just happened?

The overall look of a web page can be enhanced by properly using a color scheme. You just explored one of the web resources from where you can choose color schemes for your new PrestaShop theme.

Time for action—Changing the main page background color

It is possible to check which CSS style is adopted for a particular element in the PrestaShop website. In case you are wondering how to view what is being controlled by which CSS lines, you can perform the following steps:

1. Go to **Tools** in your web browser toolbar and select | **Firebug** | **Inspect element**, and you will be able to inspect them by holding your mouse cursor over the element with the information on the style at the bottom of the page.

2. If you are using the Web Developer extension, go to your **Tools** browser bar | **Web Developer** | **Information** | **Display Element Information**.

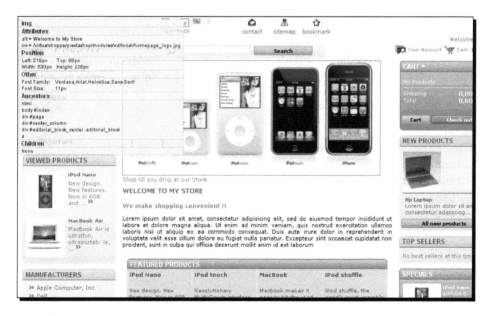

3. You will be able to see the elements information in the box, as shown in the preceding screenshot. You can move the information box by clicking and dragging it to another section of the page.

These are the two options for how to move along in our task.

Now, let's begin our task of modifying the background color of the web page.

The black area in the preceding screenshot is coded as body. The elements that you see on these areas will be changed if you modify any of the lines that define body

To change the background color of the page, look out for these lines in the global.css file:

```css
body{
    background-color: white;
    font-size: 11px;
    font-family: Verdana, Arial, Helvetica, Sans-Serif;
    color: #5d717e;
    text-align:center
}
```

What just happened?

You just explored the way to modify the background color of the pages of your website. By default, the color of the body is white, and you just changed it to black.

Changing the blocks background colors

Here we will cover how to change:

◆ The background color of default blocks such as the CATEGORIES block

◆ The background color of the exclusive blocks such as the CART block

Time for action—Changing the default blocks' background color

Let's look up the lines in the file that we need to change in order to modify the background color of the left and the right blocks; this change will affect the background color of the content of the blocks, which are considered default. They (the blocks) are:

◆ TAGS

◆ CATEGORIES

◆ VIEWED PRODUCTS

◆ MANUFACTURERS

◆ SUPPLIERS

◆ INFORMATION

◆ TOP SELLERS

◆ NEW PRODUCTS

Perform the following steps to change the background color:

1. Scroll down the `global.css` file and go to `/*Default block style*/`

```
/* Default block style */
div.block {
  margin-bottom: 1em;
  width: 191px
}
#left_column div.block, #right_column div.block{
  padding-bottom: 6px;
  background: transparent url('../img/block_footer.gif') no-repeat
  bottom left
```

```
}
div.block h4 {
  text-transform: uppercase;
  font-family: Helvetica, Sans-Serif;
  font-weight: bold;
  font-size: 1.2em;
  padding-left:0.5em;
  border-bottom:1px solid #595A5E;
  padding-top:2px;
  line-height:1.3em;
  color: #374853;
  height: 19px;
  background: red url('../img/block_header.gif') no-repeat top
  left
}
div.block h4 a { color: #374853; }
div.block ul { list-style: none; }
div.block ul.tree li { padding-left:1.2em; }
div.block a:hover { text-decoration: underline; }
#left_column div.block .block_content a.button_large, #right_
column div.block .block_content a.button_large { margin:0 0 0
-3px; }
div.block .block_content {
  border-left: 1px #d0d3d8;
  border-right: 1px #d0d3d8;
  padding:0.5em 0.7em 0pt;
  background: #f1f2f4 url('../img/block_bg.jpg') repeat-x bottom
  left;
  min-height:20px
}
div.block li {
  padding: 0.2em 0 0.2em 0em;
  list-style-position: outside
}
div.block a {
  color: #595a5e;
  text-decoration: none
}
```

2. Change the background color to the color you prefer (by changing the color code `#f1f2f4`, as highlighted in the preceding code).

You will note that some of the descriptions are linked to images. In most circumstances, for most browsers, these background images will overwrite the background colors. If you want the color to appear in any browser at the front office, you will have to delete the code on the background image, for example:

```
url('../img/block_bg.jpg') repeat-x bottom left
```

We will discuss more about background images and how they enhance your themes in *Chapter 5, Applying Images*.

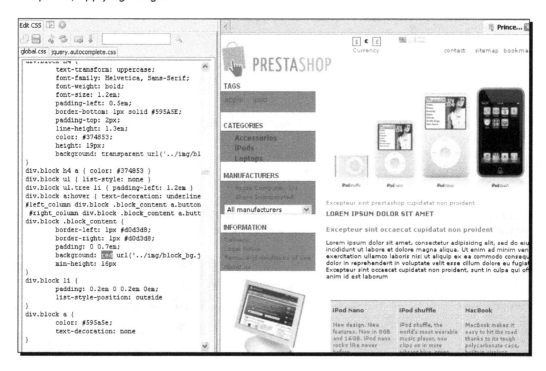

What just happened?

You just learned how to change the background color of the content for the default blocks.

Time for action—Changing the exclusive blocks' background color

Now let's go to the lines in the CSS file that we have to change in order to modify the background color of the content for cart blocks and other exclusive blocks.

Scroll down the `global.css` file and go to `/*block exclusive*/`.

```
/* block exclusive */
#left_column div.exclusive, #right_column div.exclusive {
  background: transparent url('../img/block_exclusive_footer.jpg')
  no-repeat bottom left
}
div.exclusive h4 {
  background: transparent url('../img/block_header_exclusive.gif')
  no-repeat top left;
  color: white
}
div.exclusive h4 a { color: white; }
div.exclusive li { margin-top: 0; }
div.exclusive, div.exclusive a { color: white; }
div.exclusive .block_content {
  background: #bdc2c9 url('../img/block_exclusive_bg.jpg') repeat-x
  bottom left;
  border-left: 1px solid #595a5e;
  border-right: 1px solid #595a5e
}
```

You may replace the highlighted hex color code with "red". You will note that the descriptions are also linked to an image. We will discuss it in the next chapter.

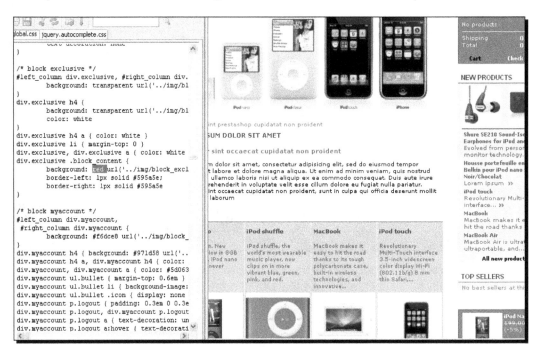

Time for action—Changing the background color of the CATEGORIES block header

The default blocks are formed by a content block and a header block.

You just learned how to modify the default block background color, but how about the header of this default block?

Let's take an example of the **CATEGORIES** block, which is one of the default blocks. There are a number of blocks which are categorized as the default blocks. They are **TAGS**, **MANUFACTURERS**, **NEW PRODUCTS**, and **TOP SELLERS**.

Every block is currently linked to the block style which is using the same header (redirected to `block_header.gif`) except those that are controlled by `block exclusive` and `myaccount`

You can change the block header background color by performing the following steps:

1. Edit these lines within the default block style:

```
div.block h4 {
  text-transform: uppercase;
  font-family: Helvetica, Sans-Serif;
  font-weight: bold;
  font-size: 1.2em;
  padding-left:0.5em;
  border-bottom:1px solid #595A5E;
  padding-top:2px;
  line-height:1.3em;
  color: #374853;
  height: 19px;
  background: transparent url('../img/block_header.gif') no-repeat
  top left
}
```

2. Change the value of the highlighted background color to red to see the difference.

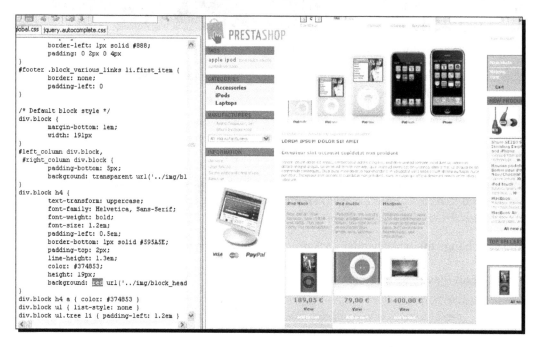

3. Now you can try your own choice of color that suits your color scheme. Once you have found the right color, you can apply the changes to your global.css file and save the changes.

Have a go hero—Making unique color for each block header

How would you make the background colors for each block headers be different from each other?

Look up the modules section in the global.css file and choose the block for which you want to change the background color.

In this example, we will add a new block style for the **INFORMATION** block header with the background color set to red

Insert the following code, which is a modified CSS of the default block style under the /* Default block style */ section.

```
/* New information block style */
div.block1 {
  margin-bottom: 1em;
  width: 191px
}
#left_column div.block1, #right_column div.block1 {
  padding-bottom: 6px;
  background: transparent url('../img/block_footer.gif') no-repeat
bottom left
}
div.block1 h4 {
  text-transform: uppercase;
  font-family: Helvetica, Sans-Serif;
  font-weight: bold;
  font-size: 1.2em;
  border-bottom: 1px solid #595A5E;
  padding-top: 2px;
```

```
    padding-left:0.5em;
    line-height: 1.3em;
    color: #374853;
    height: 19px;
    background: red
  }
div.block1 h4 a { color: #374853; }
div.block1 ul { list-style: none; }
div.block1 ul.tree li { padding-left:1.2em; }
div.block1 a:hover { text-decoration: underline; }
#left_column div.block1 .block_content a.button_large, #right_column
div.block1 .block_content a.button_large { margin:0 0 0 -3px; }
div.block1 .block_content {
    border-left: 1px #d0d3d8;
    border-right: 1px #d0d3d8;
    padding:0.5em 0.7em 0pt;
    background: #F5FEFF url('../img/block_bg.jpg') repeat-x bottom
    left;
    min-height:20px
  }
div.block1 li {
    padding: 0.2em 0 0.2em 0em;
    list-style-position: outside
  }
div.block1 a {
    color: #595a5e;
    text-decoration: none
  }
```

Save the `global.css` file once you have copied this code into the file.

In this example, this code is actually duplicated from `div.block`, and we have changed the duplicated code of the `div.block` lines to `div.block1`.

 Remember that this name, that is, `div.block1`, must be the same class name you used in the related `tpl` file, in this case, `blockinfos.tpl`.

As we choose the **INFORMATION** block as an example block to change the header color, let's now open the `tpl` file of this particular block and search for the code.

So, for the **INFORMATION** block, you will have to look up in: `/modules/blockinfos/blockinfos.tpl`

There you will see the following code:

```
<!-- Block informations module -->
<div id="informations_block_left" class="block">
  <h4>{l s='Information' mod='blockinfos'}</h4>
  <ul class="block_content">
    {foreach from=$cmslinks item=cmslink}
      <li><a href="{$cmslink.link}"
      title="{$cmslink.meta_title|escape:html:'UTF-
      8'}">{$cmslink.meta_title|escape:html:'UTF-8'}</a></li>
    {/foreach}
  </ul>
</div>
<!-- /Block informations module -->
```

Edit the `class="block"`.

```
<div id="informations_block_left"class="block1">
```

The new code should look like the following:

```
<!-- Block informations module -->
<div id="informations_block_left" class="block1">
  <h4>{l s='Information' mod='blockinfos'}</h4>
  <ul class="block_content">
    {foreach from=$cmslinks item=cmslink}
      <li><a href="{$cmslink.link}"
      title="{$cmslink.meta_title|escape:html:'UTF-
      8'}">{$cmslink.meta_title|escape:html:'UTF-8'}</a></li>
    {/foreach}
  </ul>
</div>
<!-- /Block informations module -->
```

Save the `blockinfos.tpl` file. Presto! You now have a unique header for this particular block

You can do the same for other blocks using the same method. Repeat this for all the other blocks whose header color you want to replace. For each unique header color, you will need to create a new block, for example, `block2`, `block3`, and so on.

Changing the color in the FEATURED PRODUCTS block

The **FEATURED PRODUCTS** block is the block to highlight the products you have in your store, and it is located in the center column (just below the home page logo).

In this section, we will learn how to:

- Change the color of the background of this block.
- Change the color of the tabs of this block.

Time for action—Changing the color of the background for the FEATURED PRODUCTS block

It is easy to change the **FEATURED PRODUCTS** block background color.

1. Look for the following lines in the `global.css` file:

```css
/* Special style for block products in center column */
#center_column .products_block { border: none; }
#center_column .products_block  { color: #595a5e; }
#center_column .products_block h4 { line-height: 1.3em; }
#center_column .products_block .block_content {
   background: #d0d3d8 none;
   padding:0pt
}
#center_column .products_block ul li:hover { background-color:
#bdc2c9; }
#center_column .products_block ul li {
   border-right: 1px solid white;
   border-bottom:1px solid white;
   float: left;
   clear: none;
   width:133px;
/*height:375px;*/
   background-color: #d0d3d8;
   padding: 0;
   margin-top:0
}
```

2. The sixth line (background: #d0d3d8 none;) controls the **FEATURED PRODUCTS** block background color when there is no product featured in that block. I have changed the color code and shown it in red in the front office.

3. The ninth line (background-color: #bdc2c9;) is the background color of the blocks when the mouse hovers over them. I have changed the color code and shown it in blue.

4. The nineteenth line (background-color: #d0d2d8;) is the line you should modify if you want to change the color of the **FEATURED PRODUCTS** block. I have changed the code and made it green (just to show you the difference).

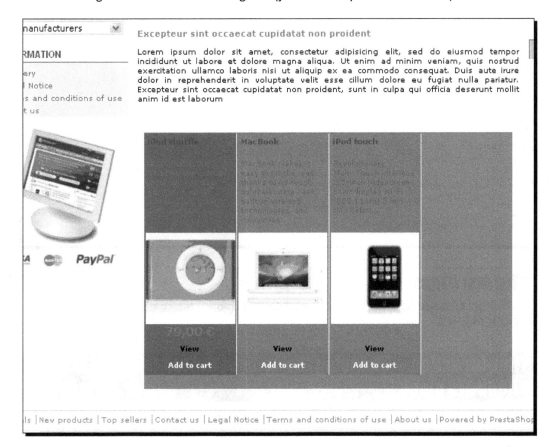

5. Always try to find the correct class and ID of the element you want to change. In this case, find: `#center_column .products_block .block_content` to change the background color to a color of your preference. The following screenshot is what you see when you use Firebug to review the `global.css` file.

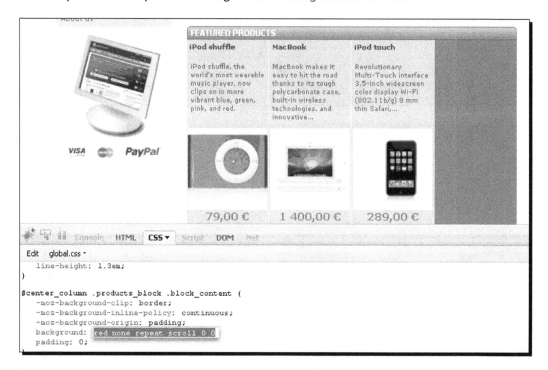

What just happened?

You have just learned how to change the background color of the content in the **FEATURED PRODUCTS** block.

Time for action—Changing the color of the tab for the FEATURED PRODUCTS block

Let's try changing the color of the tab of the **FEATURED PRODUCTS** block.

1. Look out for the following code:

```
/* block in the center column */
#center_column p { margin: 0.5em 0; padding-left:0.7em;}
#center_column div.block { width: 536px; margin:auto;}
#center_column div.block h4 {
```

```
background: transparent url('../img/block_header_large.gif') no-
repeat top left;
height: 17px;
color: white
}
```

2. Delete the URL and replace it with red. Your code should now look as follows:

```
/* block in the center column */
#center_column p { margin: 0.5em 0; padding-left:0.7em;}
#center_column div.block { width: 536px; margin:auto;}
#center_column div.block h4 {
background:    red;
height: 17px;
color: red
}
```

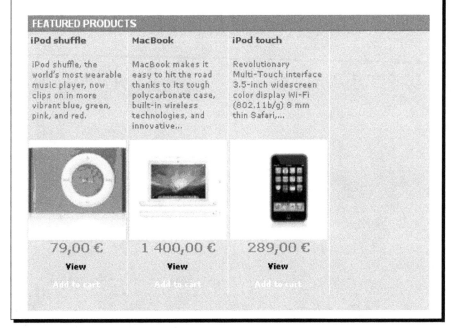

What just happened?

You have just learned how to replace the color of the tab for the **FEATURED PRODUCTS** block.

We will deal with replacing the image of the top tab for this block with another image file in the next chapter.

Time for action—Changing the background color of the footer

In order to change the background color of your footer, perform the following steps:

1. Look up for the following section in the `global.css` file.

```
/* Footer */
#footer {
   border-top: 1px solid #d0d3d8;
   padding: 0.5em 0;
   clear: both
}
```

2. Find out the hex code of your preferred background color. You may also add in the name of the color to the code.

3. It should now look like the following:

```
#footer {
   border-top: 1px solid #d0d3d8;
   padding: 0.5em 0;
   clear: both;
   background: red
}
```

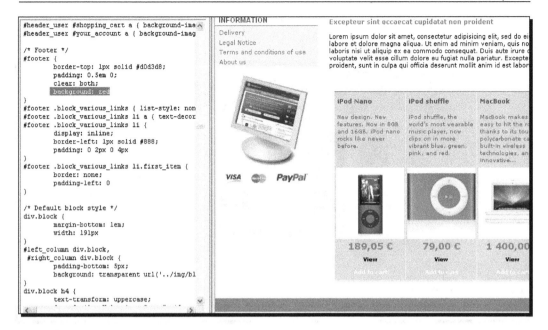

What just happened?

You just changed the background color of the footer through simple editing of the CSS file.

Time for action—Changing the header user block background color

Look out for the #header and insert background: #888 in it.

```
#header {
    float: left;
    width: 71%;
    text-align: right;
        background: #888
}
```

The color can be replaced with any color of your choice.

The following screenshot is what you will end up with. The red outline is the header section outlined by the Web Developer extension.

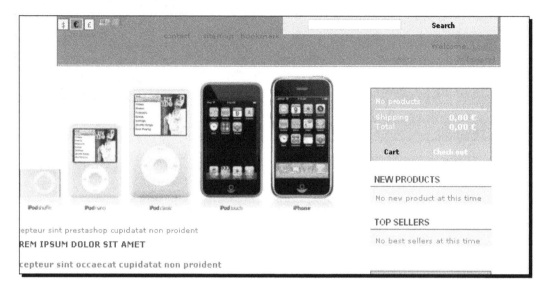

What just happened?

You just learned how to insert a hex color code in the `global.css` file to modify the header background color.

Have a go hero—Adding code in a section to change the background color

Is there a way to change the background color in one section?

Look up the CSS file and see the sections which may be modified to make it easier for you.

Looking back, there are many sections you need to dig through in the CSS file. There is an alternative route to it, but you need to be sure that you are not confusing yourself by inserting new properties into the ID selectors within the global layout section.

If you understood the manner in which you can edit the CSS file, you can also do this through the `/*global layout*/` section. Add `background: color of your choice` to the following classes.

```css
/* global layout */
#page {
  width: 980px;
  margin: 0 auto 2px auto;
  text-align: left;
  background: #C6F66F
}
h1#logo {
  float: left;
  width: 27%;
  margin-top: 0.5em
}
#header_right {
  float: left;
  margin-bottom: 15px;
  width: 73%;
  text-align: right;
  background: #C6F66F
}
#left_column, #center_column, #right_column { float: left }
#left_column {
  clear: left;
  width: 191px;
  margin-right: 21px;
  overflow: hidden;
  background:#B4F63D
}
#center_column {
  width: 556px;
  margin: 0 0 30px 0;
  overflow: hidden;
  background:#8EEB00
}
#right_column {
  width: 191px;
  margin-left: 21px;
  overflow: hidden;
  background: #82B22C
}
```

The following screenshot is what you will end up with.

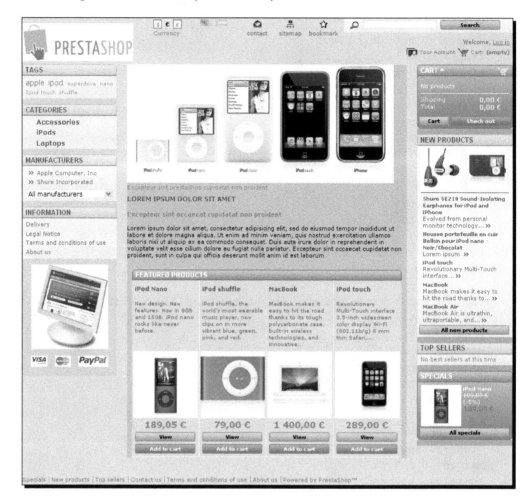

The background color for the left column, center column, and right column are coded in different shades of green. Those areas where you still see grayish colors and have not changed from the original will require further editing in the `global.css` file. Some of which are background images or background colors on various blocks which we covered in *Chapter 5, Applying Images*. Alternatively, you can add new properties in the various sections, although this will require more understanding of the CSS.

The global layout changes you made in these classes or IDs will affect the other related pages. An example of the effect will be on the product page, as shown on the next screenshot.

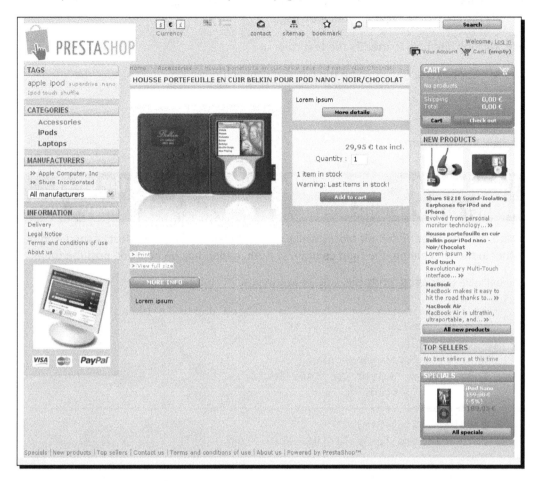

Modifying text

Text is an important element in any web page. When we modify a theme, we need to look into modifying text in terms of color, size, and type. With regards to PrestaShop, we will have to consider the various blocks or the section of a page to edit.

Changing the color of the text

If you plan to change the background color, it would also be essential to look at how to modify the color of the text in your web page.

We will look into how to modify the text color in:

- Various block headers on the left and right columns
- Footer
- Top blocks
- Center columns

Time for action—Changing the color of the text in the block header of the default blocks

There are a number of default blocks which we have identified earlier. Most of them can be either in the left column, the right column, or both, depending on how you position them.

We will pick the **CATEGORIES** block as an example.

```
Find the following code which is located under /* Default block
style */ section.
div.block h4 {
  text-transform: uppercase;
  font-family: Helvetica, Sans-Serif;
  font-weight: bold;
  font-size: 1.2em;
  padding-left:0.5em;
  border-bottom:1px solid #595A5E;
  padding-top:2px;
  line-height:1.3em;
  color: #374853;
  height: 19px;
  background: transparent url('../img/block_header.gif') no-repeat
  top left
```

We will change the default color #374853 to **red** just to show you the difference.

The following screenshot is what you will get on your screen. The left split is the CSS, which has been modified.

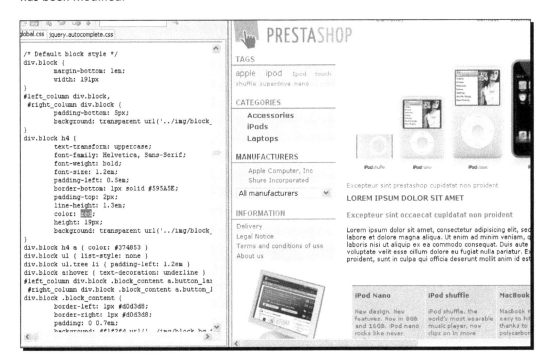

Automatically, once you change the color code, all the head text on the default blocks will change to red. Notice that the **MANUFACTURERS** block remains "gray". This is because it is being controlled by different code, which we will discuss next.

Time for action—Changing the color of the text of the header on the MANUFACTURERS block

Just below the code for the color of the text of the earlier blocks, we have the code for controlling any default-style blocks that have a link in the header.

We will use the **MANUFACTURERS** block as an example for such blocks.

The default color code was #374853. We will change the code to **green** just to show the difference.

```
div.block h4 a { color: #374853; }
div.block ul { list-style: none; }
div.block ul.tree li { padding-left:1.2em; }
div.block a:hover { text-decoration: underline; }
#left_column div.block .block_content a.button_large, #right_column
div.block .block_content a.button_large { margin:0 0 0 -3px; }
div.block .block_content {
  border-left: 1px #d0d3d8;
  border-right: 1px #d0d3d8;
  padding:0.5em 0.7em 0pt;
  background: #f1f2f4 url('../img/block_bg.jpg') repeat-x bottom
  left;
  min-height:20px
}
```

The following screenshot is the front office view based on the changes we made:

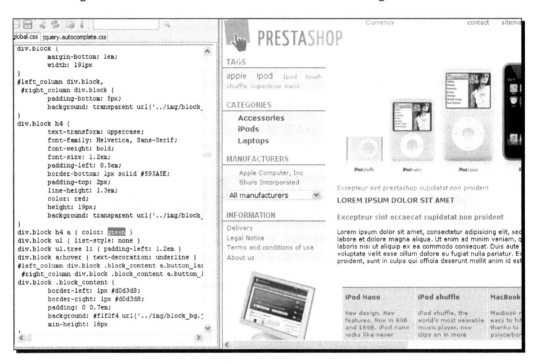

Time for action—Changing the color of the text in the exclusive blocks (CART, SPECIALS)

1. Find the following line in your CSS file: `/* block exclusive */`

2. The syntax that you need to look out for is:

```
div.exclusive h4 a { color: white; }
div.exclusive li { margin-top: 0; }
div.exclusive, div.exclusive a { color: white }
```

3. Change the color to your choice, say, green for the tab and blue for the text within the block.

4. You will be able to see the resultant front office, as indicated on the right split. The **CART** and **SPECIALS** are now in green, whereas the blocks' content text is now in blue.

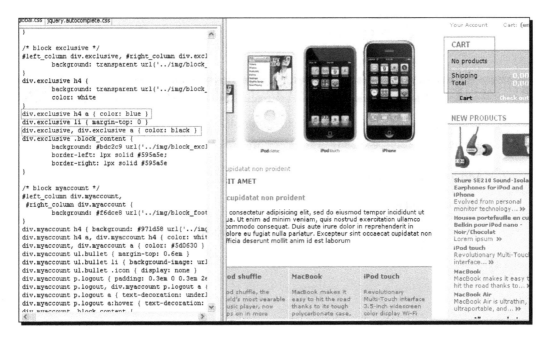

Time for action—Changing the color of the text in the top user information block

To change the color of **Welcome** text on the user block at the top-right-hand corner in the **Log in** area:

1. Look up for /* block top user information */.

2. You can then modify the code as follows, where red can be replaced with a color of your choice:

```
#header_user p { color: red }
#header_user span { font-weight: bold; }
#header_user ul { margin-top: 0.3em; }
#header_user li {
        float: right;
        line-height: 2em;
        margin-left: 0.5em;
        white-space: nowrap
}
```

Time for action—Changing the color of the text of the footer

1. To change the color of the text in the footer block, go to the global.css:

   ```
   #footer .block_various_links li a{ text-decoration:none}
   ```

2. Add a description and a value color: red.

3. Now, it should look as follows:

   ```
   #footer .block_various_links li a{ text-decoration:none;
   color:red}
   ```

The following is the CSS that appears on the screen:

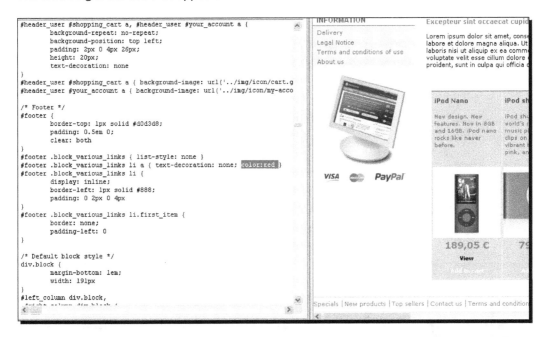

Time for action—Changing the color of the text in the center column

The color of the text in the center column, which appears under the main image, is styled by the following syntax:

```css
/* global RTE fields */
div.rte,
.mceContentBody {
  text-align:left;
  background:white;
  color:black
}
```

To change the color of the text, replace `black` with any color you want.

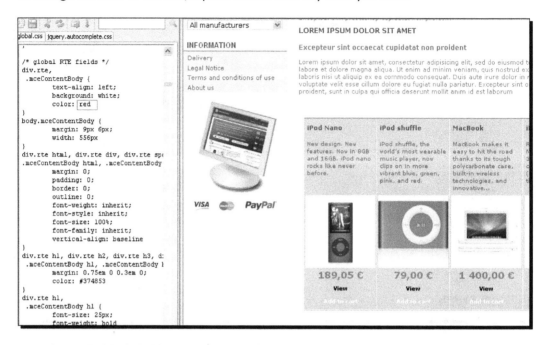

The color of the text in the **FEATURED PRODUCTS** block can be edited by looking up the `/* Special style for block products in center column */` section.

Here, we have changed the color from `#374853` to `white`.

```
#center_column div.products_block h5 a {
    color: white;
    font-size:1.1em
```

The change is shown in the following screenshot:

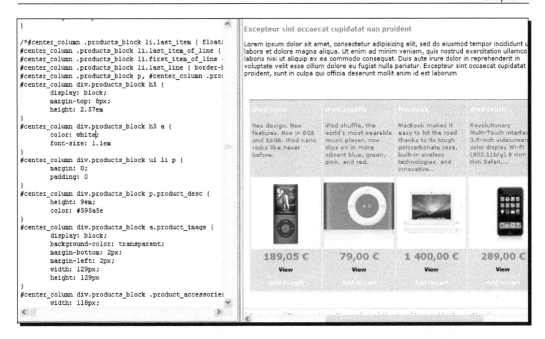

Now, change the color of the product description in the **FEATURED PRODUCTS** block.

1. Look out for this line under the /* `Special style for block products in center column` */ section.

2. Insert `color: green` into the default syntax.

3. This is how it should look, after you have inserted the new property.

```
#center_column div.products_block ul li p.product_desc a { font-
weight:normal;color: green }
```

4. The descriptions are now in green. You can try using another more visually pleasing color of your choice.

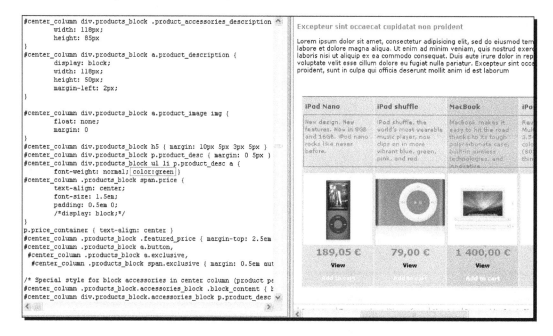

What just happened?

You have just learned how to change the color of the text in the **FEATURED PRODUCTS** block.

Time for action—Changing the color of the text in the CART block

1. The color of the text of the **CART** block can be changed through editing the following lines, which is under the `/* Special style for block cart*/` section.

2. Currently, the color of the text is `white` for both description and price in the **CART** block. To change the color of price, you have to edit `color: white` to another color of your choice.

```
#cart_block li { clear: both }
#cart_block span.price {
  color: white;
  float: right
}
```

3. In order to change the color of the description to black, go to: /* block
exclusive */, change the color to black or use a hex color code of your choice.

```
div.exclusive, div.exclusive a {
color: black}
```

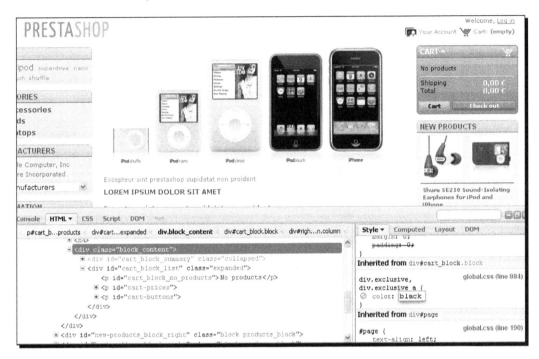

Remember we merely inserted some simple lines to the global setting to change the
background color of your pages.

Have a go hero— Changing the color of the text in the columns in one place

The same thing can be done here, but you will have to look up a different ID group within the
global setting section.

Go to the /*global layout*/. Insert the following:

color: purple for the left column, color: red for the center column, and color:
green for the right column.

The syntaxes should look like the following code:

```
#left_column, #center_column, #right_column {
  float:left
}
#left_column {
  clear:left;
  width:190px;
  padding-right: 15px;
    color: purple
}
#center_column {
  width: 556px;
  margin: 0 0 30px 0;
    color: red
}
#right_column {
  width: 190px;
  padding-left: 15px;
    color: green
}
```

This will let you change the color of the text through a simple CSS editing. As a result of your editing, the front office should look similar to the following screenshot:

We will cover most of the common concerns pertaining to the modification of text size like:

- ◆ Changing the size of the text on the default blocks
- ◆ Changing the size of the text on the center column block
- ◆ Changing the size of the text and font style on the footer blocks.

Time for action—Changing the size of the text in the default block

Changing the size of the text in the default block relate to the syntaxes we used in the previous section where we modified the background color of these blocks.

1. Get to the following syntax of the `global.css` file within the `/* Default block style */ section`, to edit the text.

    ```
    div.block h4 {
       text-transform: uppercase;
       font-family: Helvetica, Sans-Serif;
       font-weight: bold;
       font-size: 1.2em;
       padding-left:0.5em;
       border-bottom:1px solid #595A5E;
       padding-top:2px;
       line-height:1.3em;
       color: #374853;
       height: 19px;
       background: transparent u'l('../img/block_header.'if') no-repeat
       top left
    }
    ```

2. You can make the font size larger by increasing the em value in the `font-size`.

3. Normally, you wouldn't want to change it drastically due to the constraints on other related elements such as the background and the span of the block header.

This editing is only relevant to the blocks which were affected by changes made using the same syntaxes in the previous section; that is **TAGS** block, **CATEGORIES** block, **INFORMATION** block, **NEW PRODUCTS** block, and **TOP SELLER** block.

The blocks with links such as the **MANUFACTURER** block and the **CART** block are modified through a different set of syntaxes, as we have seen earlier.

What just happened?

You explored the way to change the size of the text in the default style blocks. Through this knowledge you may try to discover how to change the size of the text in the other blocks.

Time for action—Changing the size of the text and font style on the center column blocks

1. We can change the size of the text and font style on the center column block by modifying the following lines in the /* Special style for block products in center column */ section.

    ```
    #center_column div.products_block h5 a {
      color: #374853;
      font-size:1.1em
    }
    ```

2. For the font-size, we can make it smaller or bigger by adjusting the value of the em.

3. We can add an additional style by inserting a line like the following one:

    ```
    font-family: Verdana, Geneva, sans-serif;
    ```

    The following is a modified syntax:

    ```
    #center_column div.products_block h5 a {
      color: #374853;
      font-size:1.1em;
        font-family: Verdana, Geneva, sans-serif
    }
    ```

 You should always provide font backups in case the font is unavailable.

You can work on the web developer tool (for example, Firebug or Web Developer extension) to preview the changes as you edit them. If you feel happy with the changes you can then edit your file according to the changes and use this new style for your PrestaShop site.

What just happened?

You learned how to resize the size of a text element and also discovered a way to specify a font style for it.

Time for action—Changing the size of the text and font style on the footer blocks

It is possible to change the size of the text and the font style in the footer by modifying the following syntax. This is located in the footer section too. We have changed the font size to 1.3em. The default code did not specify anything here.

```
#footer .block_various_links li a{ text-decoration:none;
font-size:1.3em
}
```

What just happened?

In the previous three exercises, you learned how to change the size of the text and font of the default block, center column block, and footer block. You should be able to see a pattern and apply the knowledge in the other blocks.

Changing the color of the border

Border color is another element that we will cover in this chapter. There are various borders that can be enhanced with interesting color combination with the contents background and text color.

Here, we will cover how to:

- Change the color of the border for the default block header.
- Change the color of the border on the footer block.

Time for action—Changing the color of the border for the default block

There are other ways to make a unique looking theme. You can also play around with the color of the border of the blocks.

Let's look at an example of how we can change the color of the border within the default block, that is, the **CATEGORIES** block.

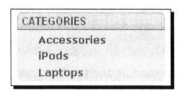

Let's start by inspecting the element through Firebug.

You can see from the preceding screenshot that the **CATEGORIES** block's `border bottom` property is stated as `border bottom: 1 px solid #595A5E`. Now let's change this to `red`.

1. The line you are looking for will be in `/* Default block style */`.

    ```
    div.block h4 {
      text-transform: uppercase;
      font-family: Helvetica, Sans-Serif;
    ```

```
  font-weight: bold;
  font-size: 1.2em;
  padding-left: 0.5em;
  border-bottom: 1px solid #595A5E;
  padding-top: 2px;
  line-height: 1.3em;
  color: #374853;
  height: 19px;
  background: transparent url('../img/block_header.gif') no-repeat
  top left
}
```

2. Change the hex color code to `red` or any other color you prefer.

```
div.block h4 {
  text-transform: uppercase;
  font-family: Helvetica, Sans-Serif;
  font-weight: bold;
  font-size: 1.2em;
  padding-left: 0.5em;
  border-bottom: 1px solid red;
  padding-top: 2px;
  line-height: 1.3em;
  color: #374853;
  height: 19px;
  background: transparent url('../img/block_header.gif') no-repeat
  top left
}
```

3. Note that even though you are just changing a default block of **CATEGORIES**, the entire site will change, as this is a style applied to all h4 selectors.

Have a go hero— Changing all the colors of the borders of the block header

Let's find out how to change the rest of the border around the block header. Open your Firebug again. Go to the CSS of the same div.block h4. Insert the following lines:

```
border-top: 1px solid green;
border-right: 1px solid blue;
border-left: 1px solid red;
border-bottom: 1px solid black;
```

The new code will look like the following:

```
div.block h4 {
    text-transform: uppercase;
    font-family: Helvetica, Sans-Serif;
    font-weight: bold;
    font-size: 1.2em;
    padding-left: 0.5em;
      border-top: 1px solid green;
      border-right: 1px solid blue;
      border-left: 1px solid red;
      border-bottom: 1px solid black;
    padding-top: 2px;
    line-height: 1.3em;
    color: #374853;
    height: 19px;
    background: transparent url('../img/block_header.gif') no-repeat
    top left
}
```

If you preview it again through Firebug, it will look like the following screenshot:

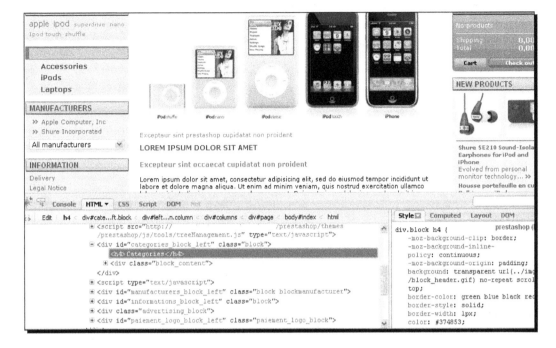

Note that the border color can also be written as:

```
border-color: green blue black red.
```

What just happened?

You modified the color of the border for the header of the blocks by using CSS properties and values.

Time for action—Changing the color of the border in the footer

To change the color of the border on the footer, look at the footer section. We will replace the `border-left` values to red.

```
#footer .block_various_links li {
    display: inline;
    border-left: 1px solid red;
    padding: 0px 2px 0px 4px;
```

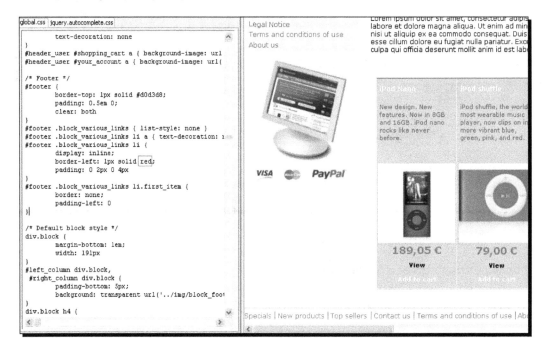

You can also modify the color of the top borders by modifying the following lines:

```
#footer {
    border-top: 1px solid red;
    padding: 0.5em 0;
    clear: both
}
```

You will get the following screenshot as a result:

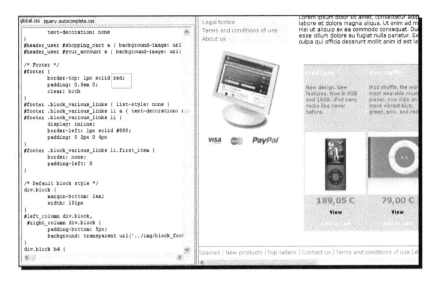

Modifying the paragraph

You may want to edit the text within the center column, but you can't do it by using the back office panel.

Time for action—Modifying lines in the center column

1. Open Firebug, and go to the element that you would like to edit.

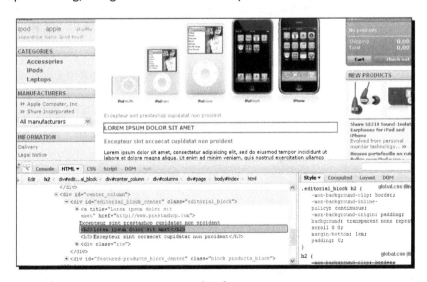

2. The text in the preceding screenshot is the text you want to edit in terms of its margin, and padding. You will need to go to global.css and edit the text sixe, padding and bottom margin.

```
.editorial_block h2 {
        background: none;
        padding: 0;
        margin-bottom: 1em
}
```

> If it isn't stated whether it is the bottom or top margin, the margin values are shown according to top right bottom left.

3. You can test how you want to change the margin and padding by increasing the value, by lowering the distance from top, and so on.

Try it, and if the outcome is suitable, you can save the changes and copy the new margin and padding value to your CSS file.

This is pretty simple!

Saving your changes

Once you have edited and modified the necessary values or syntaxes in your global.css file, you may save the file and replace the existing global.css file in the new theme folder.

Make sure you comment your changes by inserting /*   */ on the areas you modify, so if you need to review it again, you will be able to track any modifications you or your colleague made to the file.

Summary

You have learned how to modify quite a number of elements in your PrestaShop site using CSS.

More specifically, covered:

- How to look up color schemes
- The basis of CSS and applying the knowledge in modifying the PrestaShop theme.
- How to modify background color in various sections.
- How to modify the text color, size, and font in various sections.
- How to modify the border color of the blocks.

Now that you've learned about making basic changes to your PrestaShop theme, we will move onto the next chapter to learn about another important element, which is the images and background images. This is an important aspect in PrestaShop. As you can see, PrestaShop is quite "heavy" on using background images in its theming.

5
Applying Images

There are many ways to make your theme more attractive and unique. It can be done through applying some simple techniques. Based on the modifications you made in the global.css file earlier, you may have already created a unique theme.

You can change the look of the themes further by adding or replacing the default images with new images you created or obtained from various web resources. This chapter elaborates on applying the images, particularly background images, to complete the look of the theme for your online store.

Firstly, we will learn how to change the background images by editing the CSS. We will also explore how to modify the correct lines in the appropriate section of the CSS file.

Then let's look at replacing a couple of the default background images and see what effect this has on the overall design. We will show how to view the image information and then figure out what to replace or change. For this exercise, we will insert images through the global.css file. Later, we will also have to edit some other files, depending on where the relevant code are.

We will then add new images to areas which, in the default theme, do not currently have any background images.

In order to add a new background image, if you have little understanding of how CSS works, just follow these steps and you will be able to modify the background images used on the particular elements. You will need to repeat these steps on the other pages if there are other elements with background images.

Editing CSS to modify background images

You may have not realized that a lot of impact is made by the images you use on your PrestaShop store. If you change the color of the block headers, you get a new look. Add more dramatic background patterns to your page, and you may change the feel of your entire site to something else.

Although there are no rights or wrongs in designing and designs are always subjective, there are conventions and common concepts that you may use in dealing with images on your site. It would be quite strange to use colorful zany looking images for professional business concerns. You may end up presenting the wrong image to your audience by using the wrong "image" in your website!

Notice that in PrestaShop default theme, the blocks headers make extensive use of background images. They create a "fuller" or 3-dimensional look to the blocks, which would otherwise look flat.

In most e-commerce systems, the content is separated from the layout. In some systems, the CSS styles facilitate rounded corners for blocks. However, in many cases, the trouble is with the browser, some browsers do not support using CSS for rounded corners, while other browsers do support this CSS feature.

To avoid this problem where different browsers show a different look for your theme blocks, it is much easier to use corner images as background images. This is one of the reasons you will notice that most of the rounded blocks you see on the default theme use background images as PrestaShop has not built any code to feature rounded corners.

Time for action—Viewing image information

1. We can view through your Firefox Web Developer tool or Firebug and get an idea about the background images you may have to replace if you are developing a new theme.

2. Go to **Tools | Web Developer | Image | Outline Images | Background Images**.

There are plenty of background images you need to change to get a new look. Some are used in the block header and others are used in the block content, and so on. The preceding screenshot shows all the background images on the front page of your site. The images outlined in red are all the images but you can only see them as accent to the site. The background image elements that you may consider replacing can be some or all of the following:

- Backgrounds
- Banners
- Bullets
- Buttons
- Icons

To find out the location of a background image:

1. Move your mouse over the image you want to check.

2. Right-click the image. You will see the menu option **View Background Image**.

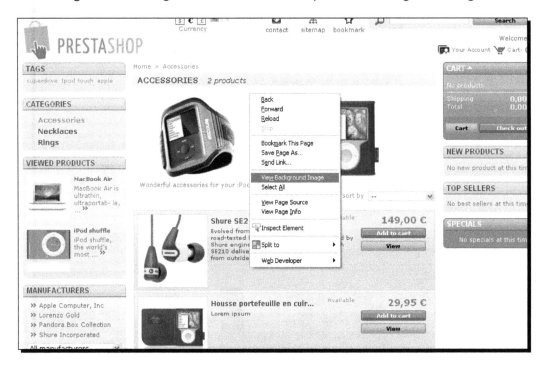

3. Click that option and you will be directed to a page where the image will be shown individually. The path to the image on your server will be displayed in your browser's address bar.

4. This is where the example background image is located: `http://www.yoursitename.com/prestashop/themes/theme1/img/block_category_item_bg.jpg`

5. Notice that it is in the `img` folder of the theme being used (that is, `theme1`).

6. You can right-click on the image you see and download it to edit it. Alternatively, you can always edit the file using a copy of the image that you made when you downloaded Prestashop, as long as you know which item you want to edit and which one you want to keep as it is.

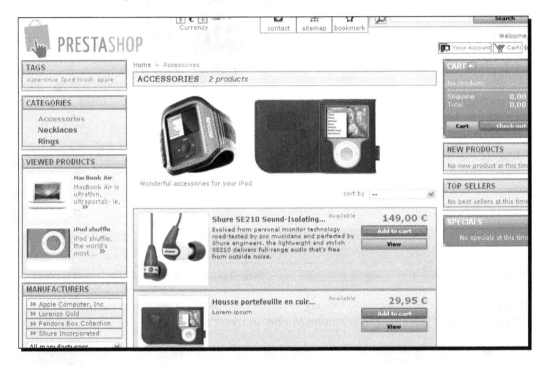

7. Although the example show use of the Web Developer extension, you can also use Firebug to view the path of the images. These tools were explained in the previous chapter).

By doing this, you will have some idea when you upload an image for the products catalog where the images will appear. When you want to replace an image or a background image, it is necessary to know what to replace or change and know where the files are located within the PrestaShop directory.

In the above screenshot we used Firebug to inspect the background image element for the Categories block. The image information can be seen on the right split.

Time for action—Finding the appropriate images

1. Find a suitable image you would like to see on that particular page. You may not know the exact dimensions of the image that you want to replace. You may need to crop or resize it.

 If you are getting images through the Internet, be careful about infringing copyright ownership. You may get images legally through subscription to stock photos, getty images, and so on, but be aware of the terms and conditions of use as they can vary.

2. Choose the appropriate image you want to use. Save it to your computer's hard disk.

There are various sites that feature free background images for public use.

You just need to search "free background images" and more than 162,000,000 results will appear (at the time of writing).

Some of the good resources are as follows:

http://www.allfreebackgrounds.com/background_select.html

http://www.fg-a.com/backgrounds.htm.

http://www.grsites.com/textures/

http://www.backgroundlabs.com/

http://www.designedtoat.com/backgroundsmain.htm

http://www.free-backgrounds.com/backgrounds

Some of these resources allow you to use their design package set, which comprises those image elements that give a certain look to your theme design. This will help you shorten the time for designing icons, banners, and so on. However, it is not easy to find ones you will like. If you are good with designing these elements and selecting complimentary colors, you may want to design the individual elements from scratch.

Always check the terms of usage when downloading and using any images from any websites even if they claim to be free. You need to be extra careful and read the terms properly.

Time for action—Basic CSS editing for modifying background images

We chose one image to show how CSS can be edited to modify the background images.

Now that you have created a background with your image editor or chosen from one of the resources, you can carry on with the following steps:

1. Upload the image you had chosen to the `img` folder of your new PrestaShop theme directory. The following is the image we will use for this exercise, and it is referred to as "myimage.jpg":

2. Go to your `global.css` file. Find the element you want to add the image to. In this case, the `body` element:

```
body {
    background-color: white;
    font-size: 11px;
    font-family: Verdana, Arial, Helvetica, Sans-Serif;
    color: #5d717e;
    text-align:center
}
```

3. Insert a new line so that your code will look like the following:

```
body { background-color:white;
font-size:11px;
font-family:Verdana, Arial, Helvetica, San-Serif;
color:#5d717e;
text-align:center;
background-image:url('../img/myimage.jpg')
}
```

Repeated background image

Note that whenever you insert an image as a background using the previous method, it will automatically cover the entire page. If you do not want the image to cover the entire screen, you may use the `background-repeat` property.

Time for action—Repeating images horizontally

To repeat images horizontally, you can put the value `repeat-x` next to the `background-repeat` property.

```
body {
    background-color: white;
    background-image: url('../img/myimage.jpg');
    background-repeat: repeat-x;
    font-size: 11px;
    font-family: Verdana, Arial, Helvetica, Sans-Serif;
    color: #5d717e;
    text-align:center
}
```

The following screenshot is what you will see in your browser:

Time for action—Repeating images vertically

To repeat an image vertically, you can put the value `repeat-y` after the `background-repeat` property and separate the two properties with a semi-colon.

```
body {
    background-color: white;
    background-image: url('../img/myimage.jpg') ;
    background-repeat: repeat-y;
    font-size: 11px;
    font-family: Verdana, Arial, Helvetica, Sans-Serif;
    color: #5d717e;
    text-align:center
}
```

The patterns are now on the vertical left of the screen, as shown in the following screenshot:

Time for action—Repeating images horizontally and vertically

To repeat an image horizontally and vertically, just put the value `repeat` after the `background-repeat` property and separate the values with a colon.

```
body {
    background-color: white;
    background-image: url('../img/myimage.jpg)
    background-repeat: repeat-x: repeat-y;
    font-size: 11px;
    font-family: Verdana, Arial, Helvetica, Sans-Serif;
    color: #5d717e;
    text-align:center
}
```

The following screenshot is what you will see in your browser:

Time for action—Using image with no repetition

If you do not want an image to be repeated, just put the value `no-repeat` after the `background-repeat` property and separate them with a colon.

To avoid repetition of the image, you will need to insert the following lines:

```
body {
   background-color: white;
   background-image: url('../img/mylargeimage.jpg');
   background-repeat: no-repeat;
   font-size: 11px;
   font-family: Verdana, Arial, Helvetica, Sans-Serif;
   color: #5d717e;
   text-align:center
}
```

Normally, this applies for larger background images.

Compressing properties

It is possible to shorten the way you write your commands in CSS. If you already know your basics of the CSS compiling method for property, you will be able to add more properties through background to simplify or shorten your edited style sheet.

```
background-color: #FFFFFF;
background-image: url("file or url name");
background-repeat: no-repeat;
background-attachment: fixed;
background-position: right bottom;
```

This is already five lines of commands. To shorten the style commands, use background to incorporate the five lines, and you will get the following code:

```
background: #FFFFFF url("file or url name") no-repeat fixed right
bottom;
```

The conventions in CSS are to follow the respective arrangements:

```
[background-color] [background-image] [background-repeat] [background-
attachment] [background-position]
```

 Remember that if any of the values for the property are not given, they will be set to their default values. Always set a background-color to be used if the image is unavailable.

What to replace to get a fresh theme

Having the appropriate understanding of editing CSS for the background image modification, now let's have a look again at our global.css file.

You will notice there are quite a number of background images used. While going through the global.css file, you will notice that a number of these background images are used in the various parts of the default theme you are modifying and working on.

For the purpose of this exercise we will look into all the important background images you will need to upload to your theme1 folder. Remember, you want to create a new theme and it has to look unique.

Go to the `theme1` site (your copied default theme file) and browse the site through Firefox. View the information for the image you want to change. Next, list the background images. You can also refer to the image folder in the default theme files that you have and review each image.

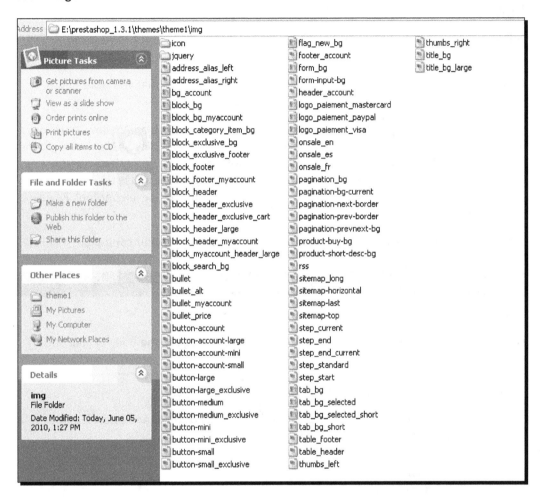

Make a list of out the images you want to overwrite.

Changing the background images for your new theme

To compare how your site will look like when you use several background images from an online resource, you can do a quick exercise by inserting the image onto the `global.css` file and review it on your web developer tool before making a decision.

Just go to your PrestaShop front office. Open your web developer tool and view the `global.css` file.

On another browser, go to a web resource for background images that you want to use. As an example, go to `http://www.free-backgrounds.com`

Choose one of the background thumbnails you'd like to review. Click on **Preview**. It will open in a new page. Then right-click on any part of the background, and click on **View background image** using Firefox. Click on that link. It will open another page: `http://www.free-backgrounds.com/backgrounds/business/bg0010.gif`. Then, Use this URL in the body of your `global.css` by inserting the code through your web developer tool. Review it in your browser.

Once you have made a choice, download the image and save it on your computer.

Time for action—Adding a background pattern

The default `background` property value for the body is `white`.

Let's change the background color and add a background image to the body of your site using the following steps:

1. Add the URL you want to use for the background image.

2. Edit the `background-color` property to the `background` and insert it in the correct section, as shown in the following code:

```
body {
   background: white;
   font-size: 11px;
   font-family: Verdana, Arial, Helvetica, Sans-Serif;
   color: #5d717e;
   text-align:center
}
```

Here we are using an 80x80 pixel square image that is used throughout as a background. The image file we used is shown in the following screenshot:

3. It is best to download the image and save it to the image (`img`) folder in your theme directory.

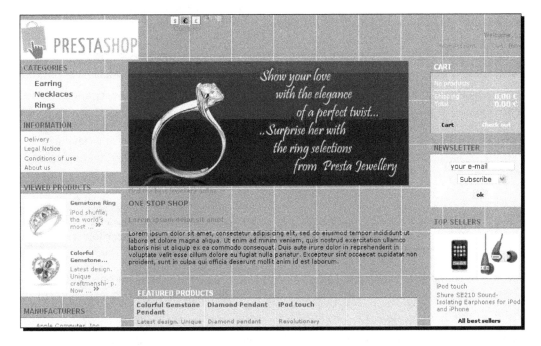

4. Edit the CSS file and change the following line:

```
background: blue url(../img/bg00012.gif);
```

5. This particular section will look like the following snippet of code:

```
body {
  background: blue url (../img/bg00012.gif);
  font-size: 11px;
  font-family: Verdana, Arial, Helvetica, Sans-Serif;
  color: #5d717e;
  text-align:center
}
```

6. When choosing the background color, you can use the eye dropper tool to match the background image color. In this way, you can get the closest match to your background image.

7. You will need to save the file and upload it to the CSS folder in the theme folder of your site. You must always check what happens after you do this by browsing through your website and reloading the pages.

What just happened?

When you decide on using a background image for a web page, there should be an alternative means for the web page to remain similar in case the image does not appear correctly in a browser. Using a background color is useful in such situations.

Time for action—Changing the block header background image

For this example, we will overwrite the eight block header files. We will now change the the the block headers from gray to red.

Then we will upload images, its best if we just use the same filenames to avoid having to edit the CSS image referencing. We will only replace the images with similar dimension and format but maintain the use of the same filenames.

 Alternatively, you can change the filenames in the global.css file according to the new image file you have uploaded to your image folder.

Let's try to change the background image of the block headers to red color background image. You don't want to use a flat color, so you need to integrate a background image to these blocks.

Firstly, to change, you will need to identify the name of the background image used in the block header. To help you minimize the time to identify the names of the background images, the easiest method is to use Firefox and just right-click on the image you want to check the background image.

If you are using IE, you may need to save the file if you cannot view it in a new browser window.

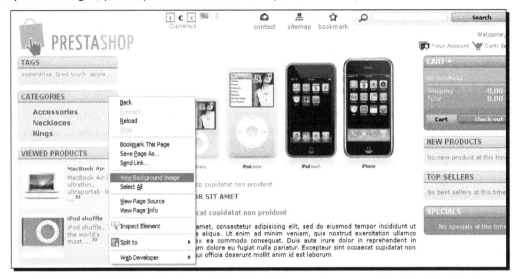

You must know the background image names in order to get the right result. The blocks in the left column are all using `block_header.gif`. The right column is quite tricky, as there are several background images and the images are all being used. The files have different names similar in shapes and colors. The special block background image uses a different filename, although the dimension and colors are the same as another background image.

In this example, we have uploaded the modified versions of:

- `block_header.gif`
- `block_header_exclusive.gif`
- `block_header_exclusive_cart.gif`
- `block_header_large.gif`

Always maintain the size of the image if you are only concerned about changing the color of the background image. This method reduces your need to look up the CSS code to modify the names of files you want to use for the blocks.

An alternative method in dealing with the block background image is by editing the `.css` file and changing the name of the image file to one that you want to use. Look up the `/*Default block style */` section in the `global.css` file.

If you are uploading a new image, which is referred to as `new_block_header.gif`, you will need to change the name of the `gif` file accordingly.

```
div.block h4 {
    text-transform: uppercase;
    font-family: Helvetica, Sans-Serif;
    font-weight: bold;
    font-size: 1.2em;
    padding-left:0.5em;
    border-bottom:1px solid #595A5E;
    padding-top:2px;
    line-height:1.3em;
    color: #374853;
    height: 19px;
    background: transparent url('../img/new_block_header.gif') no-repeat
top
    left
}
```

This will only replace the block header which used the `block_header.gif` as the background image in the default theme.

We know that the background color is transparent, with the background image in the `new_block_header.gif`, not repeating and the image positioned at the top-left of the element. You will have to repeat the process in order to change the rest of the background images used in the blocks.

Have a go hero—Replacing image in the blocks

Let's try to replace the background content of the default blocks (for example, the **CATEGORIES** block) with the new background. We will use a darker tone in this example. In order to do that, perform the following steps:

1. Identify the background image used for the block through the Firebug tool.

2. There are three background images that you need to replace:

❑ `block_bg.jpg` for the block's content

❑ `block_header.gif` for the block header

❑ `block_footer.gif` for the block's footer

3. Create a similar sized image for each of them, but use a different tone for the new background image. Upload it to the server to the `img` theme folder.

4. Overwrite the `block_bg.jpg` file in your `theme1` (new theme) file. It should go to the following folder: `/themes/theme1/img`.

5. Replace the header block. Replace the `block_header.gif` by uploading the new file and overwriting the old file. Once uploaded, review it in your browser. You will see something similar to what is shown in the following figure:

6. Replace the `block_footer.gif`. Use the new background file you just created. Upload it and overwrite the existing `block_footer.gif` file.

7. Preview it in your browser, the changes have been incorporated for these blocks.

8. All the blocks which are styled the same way in CSS will follow this new background color, except for the **NEW PRODUCTS** block, which can be problematic as it tends to grow longer because you have more items loaded in it.

9. The background color for the block should be changed accordingly, so that when the **NEW PRODUCTS** block expands, the block doesn't look unfinished, as shown in the preceding screenshot.

10. Go to `global.css` and find `/*Default block style*/`

```
div.block h4 a { color: #374853 }
div.block ul { list-style: none }
div.block ul.tree li { padding-left: 1.2em }
div.block a:hover { text-decoration: underline }
#left_column div.block .block_content a.button_large,
 #right_column div.block .block_content a.button_large { margin: 0
 0 0 -3px }
div.block .block_content {
   border-left: 1px #d0d3d8;
   border-right: 1px #d0d3d8;
   padding: 0 0.7em;
   background: #f1f2f4 url('../img/block_bg.jpg') repeat-x
   bottom left;
   min-height: 16px
}
```

11. Replace the background color code with one that is suitable for the new background image you have used:

```
div.block .block_content {
  border-left: 1px #d0d3d8;
  border-right: 1px #d0d3d8;
  padding: 0 0.7em;
  background: #bdc2c9 url('../img/block_bg.jpg') repeat-x
  bottom left;
  min-height: 16px
}
```

 Be careful when you edit the CSS commands, make sure the file format is used exactly as the name of the file and in the same lowercase or uppercase(gif and GIF are not the same in the case of images).

When you change the background color, always see what effect it has on your text as well. In such a case, you will have to modify the text color, which can be difficult to read once you have a darker background. We had learned how to change the color of the text in the previous chapter.

What just happened?

You explored the ways to change the background image and color of the blocks in the PrestaShop theme. You can use this to further modify the other background images too.

Adding a new logo

You have also learned how to add a new logo using the back office. There is another method where you can add the logo by editing a CSS file, especially if you want to modify the value of the property of the logo.

Time for action—Replacing logo using the header.tpl file

You already got yourself familiar with the CSS files. Now, we are moving on to another important file that you may have to use to edit, as an alternative from your back office.

The logo can be replaced by uploading it through the server into an appropriate folder ('../img/logo.jpg'). It's best if you can overwrite the original file using a different file with the same filename.

1. Look up your `/theme1/header.tpl`

```
<!-- Header -->
  <div>
    <h1 id="logo"><a href="{$base_dir}"
    title="{$shop_name|escape:'htmlall':'UTF-8'}"><img
    src="{$img_ps_dir}logo.jpg" alt="{$shop_name|escape:'htmlall':
    'UTF-8'}" /></a></h1>
    <div id="header">
      {$HOOK_TOP}
    </div>
  </div>
```

2. `logo.jpg` is the filename for the logo on your top-left corner. Changing the logo picture can also be done by modifying this file to the filename of the new logo, say `logo2.jpg`.

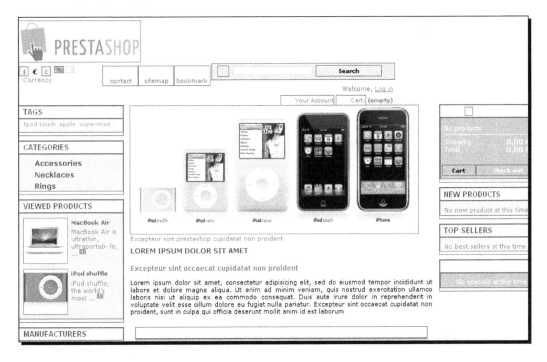

3. To edit the logo properties on the top–left, you may look up for the following lines in your `global.css` file again

```
/* global layout */
```

4. The default width for the logo is 29 percent. Changing the value to 80 percent will make the logo area wider and bring the top links to the bottom of the logo area (**contact**, **sitemap**, **bookmark**, and search blocks).

```
h1#logo {
  float: left;
  width: 80%;
  margin-top:0.5em
}
```

Positioning background image

There are a few ways to position the background image. You can use the `background-position` property with values that are in pixels, relative positions, and percentages. In PrestaShop, most of the syntaxes used are based on relative position.

As an example, a header link uses `top center` in this property.

```
#header_links a {
  display: block;
  height: 15px;
  color: #595a5e;
  padding-top: 19px;
  text-align: center;
  text-decoration: none;
  background-repeat: no-repeat;
  background-position: top center;
  background-color: transparent
}
```

 You can learn more about positioning at: `http://www.w3schools.com/css/tryit.asp?filename=trycss_background-position`

Pop quiz

How would you specify the following values for the `background position` property?

1. value positions the image 5 centimeter from the left and 10 centimeter down the page

2. value positions the image one quarter horizontally and centrally down the page

3. value positions the image at the top-left corner of the page

Modifying the home page logo

In Prestashop, the home page logo refers to the central image in the main page. You have already replaced the home page logo through the back office. However, there are situations when you may want to do more than just replace the image of this central feature of your site.

Time for action—Deleting the home page logo

1. If you do not want any image to appear in this section, go to:

`/modules/editorial/homepage_logo.jpg`.

2. You will have to delete this file.

Time for action—Replacing the home page logo

Normally, it will be easier to edit the home page logo from the back office rather than editing the files on the server.

If it is not possible to perform the required changes through the back office, we can perform the following steps:

1. Go to the `modules` folder: `/modules/editorial/`.

2. You will have to delete the `homepage_logo.jpg` file and then upload the new home page logo using the same name.

3. However, if you would like to add a file of another format, you will need to change the name of the file to the filename you used, for example, `new_homepage_logo.gif`.

4. Keep in mind that the center column width is 556 px. If you use a wider image, it will need more adjustment in your other elements.

5. The section you need to edit in the `global.css` file is `/* global layout */`.

```
#center_column {
  width: 556px;
  margin: 0 0 30px 0
}
```

Replacing icons

Another task that is related to images used in PrestaShop, which can affect your theme, is the icon set that you use. The default icons that come with the PrestaShop software are not that bad, but if you are trying to create a new theme, it can enhance your uniqueness. The icon files for the specific themes are located at: `/themes/theme1/img/icon`.

Note that `theme1` is a name that I created, you can always look into the default PrestaShop theme file or theme name if you have copied the default theme directory.

One method you can use is copying another icon set from another theme that you copied or downloaded. By pasting it into your new theme's folder, you can get a different theme with a different icon. You can also mix and match by adding or deleting some of the icons you want to use or replace if you have more theme icons that you can pick and choose from.

Another method you can use is by searching for icon sets online and just replace those that you don't want. This is quite a hassle, but the outcome will be much more customized as per your needs.

Of course, another alternative is to create icon sets from scratch and upload them to replace the ones you do not want. However, that can take a while, especially if you do not have the resources (time, effort, and human power) to create or design them.

The second and third methods are almost similar in terms of execution. The first method is simple and straightforward.

Time for action—Replacing selected icons

The icons that are quite dominant in the user's browser are:

- `cart.gif`
- `contact.gif`
- `my-account.gif`

- search.gif
- sitemap.gif
- star.gif

Let's see an example of how to replace the contact.gif icon:

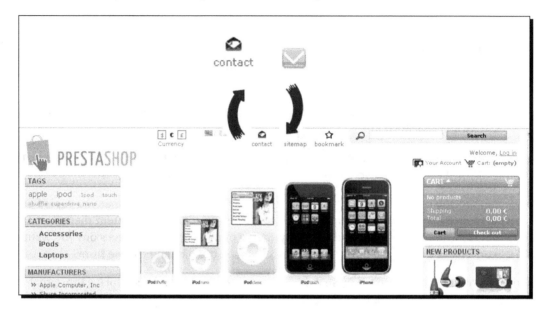

1. The icon to be used is 24x24 px, as shown in the following image and name it the same as your contact.gif:

2. Upload this file to your theme's icon folder /themes/theme1/img/icon and overwrite the existing contact.gif file.

3. Preview the changes in your browser.

4. This is it. If you don't see it, it is most likely because you have not changed your setting to the new theme in the back office. Go back to **Preference | Appearance** and choose the theme1 under the radio button option in **Themes**.

Time for action—Replacing the default icons with another icon set

This is quite tough at this point as there are not many free PrestaShop themes you can find with unique icons to copy from. However, if you do find one that you like, you can always perform the following steps to replace the entire icon set.

1. As an example, download another theme to your computer.

2. Now, go to your server and delete the icon folder in the PrestaShop directory:/ themes/theme1/img/icon.

3. Browse through your computer where you stored your new theme (say, theme2) directory.

4. Copy the icon folder (compress it) and upload the compressed archive file to your server where the icon folder was deleted.

5. Extract the archived folder and now you have a new icon folder with the theme2 icons.

6. Refresh your browser, and you should be able to see the new icon set in your web pages.

Have a go hero—Replacing all icons using your own

The most unique themes can be developed with your own design. But make sure the design is intuitive enough that site visitors will understand what you mean by an icon. If you simply change an icon for the sake of changing, it will be a disaster. Note that most people can now relate to certain icons without even a word written or used with it. For example, when you want to use a new "Contact Us" icon, do not put a "Home" icon on it as that would confuse your visitors.

You can use any of the image editors such as Paint, Photoshop, or Illustrator to create an icon. There are a number of sites claiming they have a program to create icons, but none of them work well.

Alternatively, you can also get some ideas from the following sites, some require payment, but a few offer freebies:

◆ http://www.iconspedia.com/
◆ http://www.perfect-icons.com/
◆ http://www.iconshock.com/professional-icons.php
◆ http://www.freeiconsweb.com/
◆ http://iconfactory.com/freeware/icon
◆ http://mintywhite.com/customize/icons/high-quality-free-icon-sets/
◆ http://stockicons.com/

 Always check the terms or conditions when using any downloaded copyrighted material as they always come with special terms of use for commercial sites.

If you plan to create your own icons, go to the icon folder and replace all the icons with the new ones that you have created.

It's best to use the similar sized icons (16x16) of the `gif` format. The ideal size of the icons in PrestaShop is 16×16 pixel. The larger ones can be made at 24×24 pixels.

Once completed, upload the new icon set to your server and overwrite your `theme1` (new theme directory) icon set at the specified location: `/themes/theme1/img/icon`.

What just happened?

We just learned how we can change the look of your site by replacing the icons selectively by changing a particular icon's filename to the same name as the icon it is replacing, in the theme's icon folder.

We also covered how to copy a folder to replace the default icon folder on the server so that we can use another theme's icon.

We finally learned about some resources to create icons and purchase some readymade icon packs. Unfortunately, until this point of time, we have not seen a dedicated icon pack for PrestaShop themes, so we may have to create unique themes on our own.

Summary

In retrospective, we have learned:

- The importance of background images to your theme design
- How to edit the relevant CSS lines to replace or add background images
- How to use alternative methods to edit the images and the background images
- The alternative methods to position the image on the screen

In our previous chapters, we had learned the ropes on how to modify the parts in the PrestaShop site, mostly through the back office panel and modification in some areas within the files. In the next chapter, we will learn about the steps involved in creating your own theme.

6
Steps for Creating Themes

It is possible that you might come up with a wonderful looking theme without doing the underlying work, but it is useful to know more if you want to attempt more challenging themes.

Some of this information is discussed in different chapters in greater detail, for example, we have already discussed how to get images for your PrestaShop site. However, one can stick to the flow without diverting to the other chapters too much.

Now, let's get some understanding of the PrestaShop architecture, which will be useful in order for you to make changes on the files within the directories.

This chapter provides step-by-step instructions for how to create a theme. It is divided into sub-topics such as visualizing the theme and deciding the key features and functions, creating the folder for the new theme, and modifying the CSS files to suit your PrestaShop store's concept to achieve your theming goals.

We will also learn about the PrestaShop architecture, the philosophy behind it, and get acquainted with some of the key files that affect the output of your inputs.

Understanding PrestaShop architecture

PrestaShop is based on the MVC architecture. What does this mean to you as a designer?

Here's a simple explanation of this **Model-View-Controller** (**MVC**) architecture.

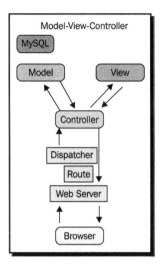

MVC is a design pattern used in software engineering for applications that require data to be maintained in multiple views. It separates the application logic of the user from what is being input or presented. It is therefore possible to separately carry out development, testing, and maintenance on each part.

An example of how the MVC operates can be seen in a situation where a site user keys in information to the relevant field on your e-commerce site, say, the products he/she wanted to purchase in the shopping cart and then he/she updates the information. When the site user chose an item and keyed in the purchase into his shopping cart; this click, which is also commonly done through a Graphical User Interface (GUI), will be transmitted to the view and the model.

In the background, the controller relays the action to the model. This results in a change in the model's state. The model will then manage this information and updates the data. In MVC, there is no specific information about data access (for example, SQL database), but it is commonly understood that it is covered by the model. Then, upon updating the data, the model has changed its state and it transmits the information so that the relevant views will be shown on the web page when it is refreshed.

The view translates these updates from the model where a site user interacts with the elements on the web page. This will update the information on the cart as it can be seen through the web browser by the site user.

These cycles happen every time a site user interacts with the GUI or the element on the web pages.

A good explanation about MVC can be obtained from various sites such as:

```
http://www.enode.com/x/markup/tutorial/mvc.html
http://java.sun.com/blueprints/patterns/MVC.html
http://st-www.cs.illinois.edu/users/smarch/st-docs/
mvc.html
```

If you examine the standard PrestaShop directory, you will note the PHP scripts within the root folder. These are basically the controller for the PrestaShop site you build. The theme, or how the PrestaShop store looks, depends on which theme is applicable and the theme folders and files set within the directory.

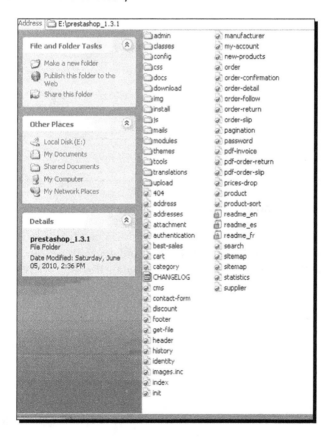

Now, let's take a look at the theme directories.

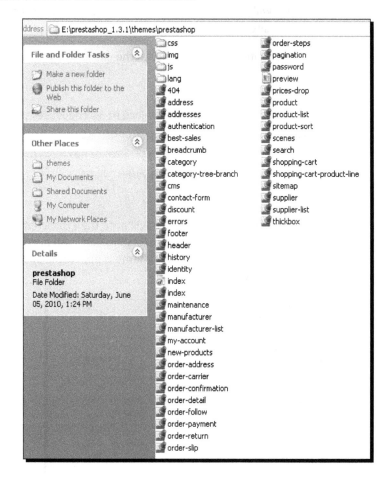

The preceding screenshot shows the files and folders within the `prestashop` default theme.

If you look up your `prestashop` directory that you download from the PrestaShop site, you will see a folder called `themes`. Go into this folder, and you will see another folder called `prestashop` inside this folder, there you will find folders like `css`, `img`, `js`, and `lang`. Until PrestaShop v1.3.0, there was another folder named `config`.

You will also see a number of `.tpl` files plus an `index.php` file within the `themes` directory.

Enough with the theory, now let's get on with our mission: to create a new theme for PrestaShop in a simple way.

Here, we will cover the following:

- Visualizing what you need in your PrestaShop theme
- Finding a similar theme to use (if any)
- Creating a file system
- Creating a new theme directory
- Copying the basic theme
- Editing the theme's `global.css` file
- Making the new theme unique

Visualizing what you want to achieve

You will need to visualize your end result. Let's start with the aim to create a theme with one column on the main page.

First, how would you get ideas for theming for PrestaShop? Get a blank piece of paper and scribble to make it easier for you to work on your mission. If you need some ideas, search for some nice websites and get the idea on paper.

Start with `http://www.prestashop.com`. There is a live showcase of PrestaShop stores that were built by the other users all over the world (we talked about this in the first chapter).

There are some other websites you can search from where you can get ideas. Here are a couple of them:

- `http://www.Prestashopthemes.net`
- `http://www.templatepresta.com/`

Once you get some idea of what you want, you can scribble it on paper to figure out the elements you may want to include and so on.

For this exercise, we will have a large home page logo image as a center image. We will have all the modules we chose as a top menu link and we do not want any products featured at the bottom. We may have an area to add some content at the bottom.

This looks quite challenging, as the main page we want to build is quite different from the standard PrestaShop layout with three columns with left and right columns plus the featured products block in the center column at the bottom. But no worries, as you will find that it is a quite a simple task!

Now that you have already figured out what layout you want to end up with, consider the concept you want to portray in your site. Decide if you want to go for a darker color or achieve a lighter mood through the elements. You can look up the color scheme site we learned about in *Chapter 2, Customizing PrestaShop Theme Part I*.

You can then choose the color scheme of the text, background, and blocks using online color schemes.

Time for action—Choosing a color scheme

Let's choose a color scheme.

1. Go to http://colorschemedesigner.com/.

2. Here you get to choose the color models you prefer, like the following:

- ❑ **mono**
- ❑ **complement**
- ❑ **triad**
- ❑ **tetrad**
- ❑ **analogic**
- ❑ **accented logic**

3. You will be given the option to **Show Tooltips**.

4. Click on this and you will be able to see information on all the models mentioned earlier.

5. For example, move your mouse over the **analogic** model and you will see information on this in a pop out box.

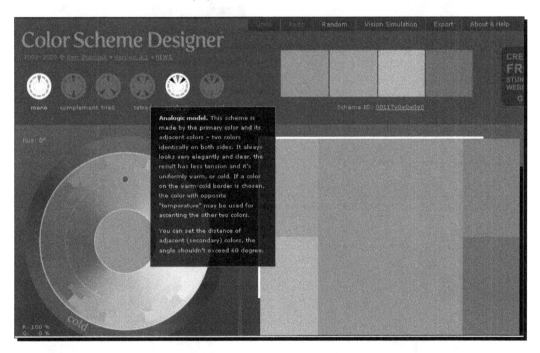

6. Let's choose a **Hue** based on a **mono** model, and you will see the following screen:

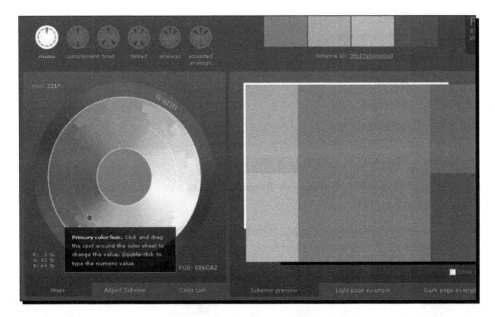

7. Adjust the scheme. Click on **Adjust Scheme** tab at the bottom.

8. Here, you will see a drop-down list that allows you to make some choices regarding the scheme.

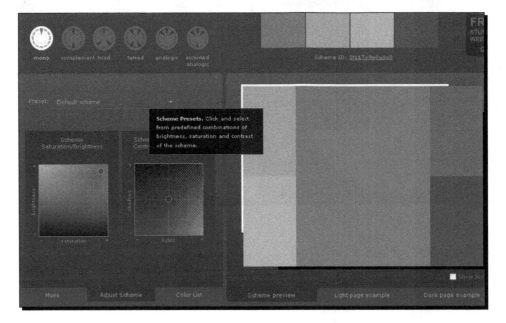

9. Choose **Pastel** from the list.

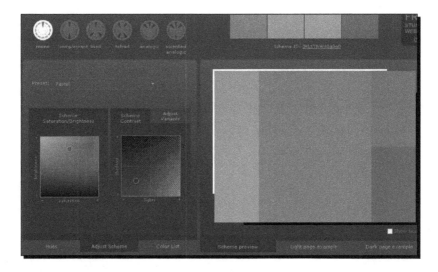

10. Click on the **Light page example** or **Dark page example** tab on the bottom right to preview the sample page.

11. You can also enable the checkbox next to the **Show text** at the bottom corner if you would like to see the sample of the page with text on.

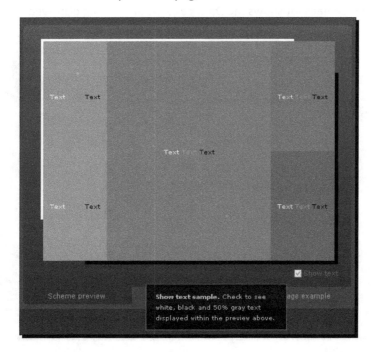

12. The following screenshot shows the **Light page** example as it appears in a new window:

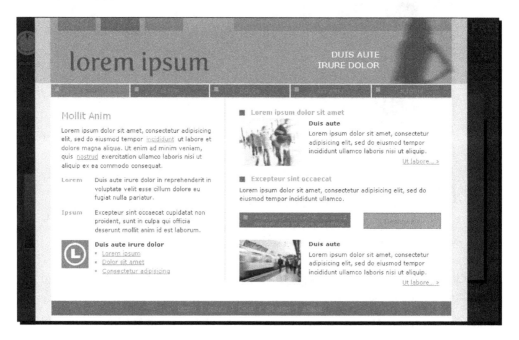

13. The next screenshot shows the **Dark page** example being displayed:

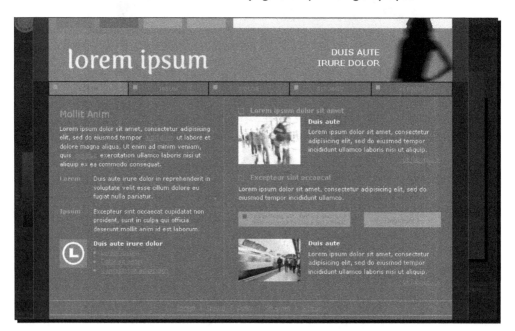

14. We will choose the **Light Pastel** as an example. You can export the color code in HTML and CSS by clicking on the **Export** button options.

What just happened?

You explored an online resource which can help you to generate and preview a color scheme for your PrestaShop store.

Have a go hero—Identifying a theme to use

There are not many free PrestaShop themes available on the net. If you failed to find one that you like, you can use the default theme as a starting point.

It will be a breeze, and you will not even have to worry about the code as you can copy and paste it without understanding it.

Okay, now we will use the default theme as the basis to work on, and as you follow the steps, you will get to the end in no time.

Time for action—Creating a new theme directory

Copy your default PrestaShop theme and name it `mytheme`.

Go to your cPanel and look up for your PrestaShop theme directory (we covered this in *Chapter 1, Customizing PrestaShop*). You should see this in your `themes` directory.

The `themes` directory path is `public_html/prestashop/themes/`, if you want to keep the prestashop folder separate or `/public_html/themes` and if you installed the content of the `/prestashop` folder to your domain (This is if you installed your PrestaShop within the root home page). In our example, we have created a sub domain where we install prestashop in a separate folder. So we have `public_html/yourdomainname/prestashop/themes/`.

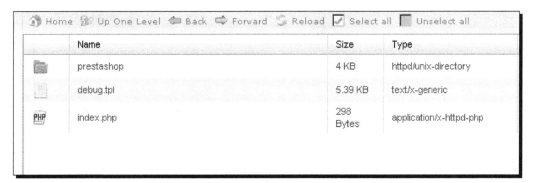

	Name	Size	Type
	prestashop	4 KB	httpd/unix-directory
	debug.tpl	5.39 KB	text/x-generic
PHP	index.php	298 Bytes	application/x-httpd-php

1. Click on the default theme folder and then copy it.

2. A pop-up window will prompt you to copy the folder to a location which is the same as the current theme file, as shown in the following screenshot. You can't copy in the same folder, so you need to create a new folder, say, "/mynewtheme/" for example, `public_html/prestashop/themes/mynewtheme`.

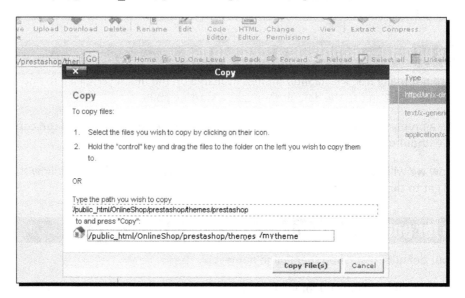

3. You will have to rename the new folder, for example, change the name to `mytheme`.

4. The following is what you should see in your `themes` directory.

5. Within this new folder, you will have exactly the same files and directory arrangement

6. Go to the back office panel of your online store.

7. Go to **Back Office** | **Preferences** | **Appearance**.

8. Scroll down to **Themes** section and choose **mytheme** by clicking on the radio button of the theme you want to apply.

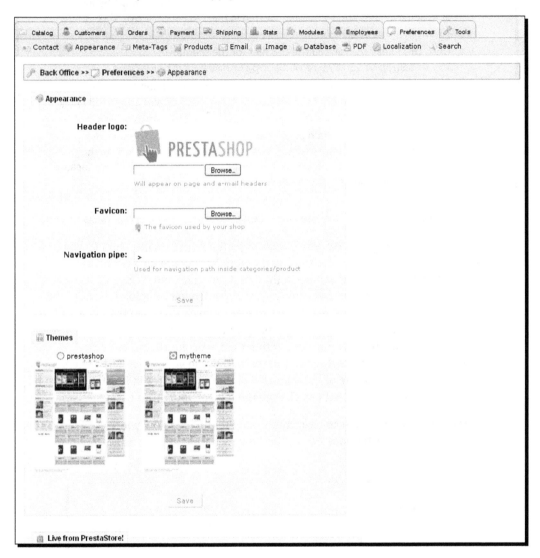

9. Click on the **Save** button. Now you have a home for your new theme. Let's begin your theming!

Note that you will have to play around a lot with these files and folders:

`img`: This folder will contain all the images needed for the template (both the folders) `/PrestaShop_1.3.1/prestashop/img` and `/PrestaShop_1.3.1/prestashop/themes/mytheme` must be looked at as some images are, by default, located in the `/PrestaShop_1.3.1/prestashop/img` folder.

`css`: This folder contains all the CSS files for the theme. `/PrestaShop_1.3.1/prestashop/themes/mytheme/css`.

`Modules`: This folder will contain modules for the PrestaShop site. Here, you can override existing modules with your changes. You can also copy third party modules into this folder `/PrestaShop_1.3.1/prestashop/modules`.

`tpl` files : `.tpl` files contain page-specific template system. The various `tpl` files are located within the folders `/PrestaShop_1.3.1/prestashop/themes/mytheme`. The modules have their own `.tpl` files which are located within the particular modules folders.

10. The front office should show the same default theme, which is our basis of working.

11. Before you do anything else, you should copy the `modules` directory to your `mytheme` as well. Most of the third party modules worked well with this arrangement. However, if you use a third party module and it doesn't show in the `Modules` page in your back office, you will still need to upload them to the `/prestashop/modules/` folder, as some of them do not have the necessary Smarty code (modules that have the required code will be displayed even if you create a new directory for modules within the particular theme directory). We will learn more about using tested third party modules in your PrestaShop site in the next chapter where some of the standard or default features in PrestaShop can be replaced with elements that can change the look of your store easily.

12. Copy the `modules` folder to your `mytheme` directory. So now you will have a module folder, which is located within the new theme `/prestashop/themes/mytheme/modules/`.

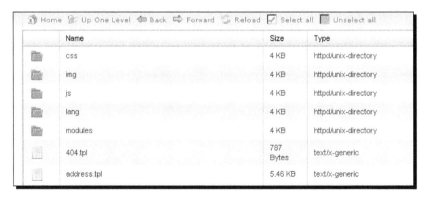

13. This will make it easier if you need to make any changes to the `modules` files without disturbing the original `modules` file. Now, disable all the modules, using the method we learned previously.

14. Go to the **Back Office | Modules** and put a check in all the boxes next to the enabled modules and disable them in one go by clicking on **Uninstall the selection** at the bottom of the page.

15. Once this is done, you can start working on a blank page for the new theme.

16. Next, navigate back to the **Back Office | Modules**, and let's start with a step further.

Your new template is now enabled and ready to be customized. You will work on a mission to create a theme without necessarily knowing what the code means. Later, we can move on to getting acquainted with what happens in the background when you modify the files that have an impact on your theme.

Developing the raw material

Consider how much a revamp can do in terms of small things such as buttons, icons, or tabs, as we have seen in *Chapter 5, Applying Images*. These are mostly the background images that you need to look up in the `img` folder. The references for these images are mostly within the `global.css` file, but as it is a large file, so you will have to go section by section.

We have gone through some of these in the previous chapters as well. We also learned how to view it using Firebug or the Web Development extension for Firefox.

On top of these, make sure you have taken sufficient pictures of your own products to be listed in the products' images. It is best if you tabulate this information and make a checklist of them.

Now, let's assume you want to create a PrestaShop store dealing with online florists.

The steps we will cover next would be:

◆ Replacing the home page logo.

◆ Creating the top horizontal menu bar.

Once you have identified the concept of your new PrestaShop store, for example, minimalistic, modern, funky, or artistic, you need to develop the elements to be used in it. For this task, our site will be minimalistic and will use light pastel colors.

We will start with the following:

- ◆ The home page logo (banner), which is approximately 980x300 pixels (the original home page logo is 300 pixels in height, but you may adjust this according to your central image size).

- ◆ Your company logo, which can be approximately the size of the original logo, that is, 224x73 pixels (you may adjust this accordingly).

You can try to generate your own banners quickly using the following links:

- ◆ `http://www.bannerfans.com/banner_maker.php`
- ◆ `http://www.bannersketch.com/`
- ◆ `http://www.mybannermaker.com`

You may still need to take or create some images or pictures which can be added in to the banner to make it unique and relevant to your product or store theme.

You can also use common software such as GIMP, Photoshop, or Illustrator if you have a the artistic flair.

For replacing our home page logo and the main logo, the steps are covered in detail in *Chapter 2, Customizing PrestaShop Theme Part I*.

However, as the homepage logo that we are using in this example is wider than the default theme's logo, we will look at how to modify the layout of the main page in the next section.

Time for action—Modifying the layout of the main pages

Based on our specs, where we want the home page logo to be wider, we will need to do some tweaking on the layout of the main page.

We will be "getting rid" of the left and right columns from the main home page, so we will need to add some code to the `header.tpl` and `footer.tpl` pages to make it look proper.

The `header.tpl` and `footer.tpl` files that we need to edit are located at `/prestashop/themes/mythemes/`.

In order to get rid of the left and right columns in the main page, we need to insert an `if` statement in the `header.tpl` and `footer.tpl`.

header.tpl

1. Look for the following code:

```
<!-- Left -->
    <div id="left_column" class="column">
        {$HOOK_LEFT_COLUMN}
    </div>
```

2. Change it to the following:

```
{if $page_name != 'index'}
<!-- Left -->
    <div id="left_column" class="column">
        {$HOOK_LEFT_COLUMN}
    </div>
{/if }
```

3. Save the file.

footer.tpl

1. Look for the following code:

```
<!-- Right -->
    <div id="right_column" class="column">
        {$HOOK_RIGHT_COLUMN}
    </div>
```

2. Change it to the following:

```
{if $page_name != 'index'}
<!-- Right -->
    <div id="right_column" class="column">
        {$HOOK_RIGHT_COLUMN}
    </div>
{/if}
```

3. Save the file.

4. You should have both columns clear from all the blocks on the main page.

5. Now add this line to your theme's `global.css` in the `/*global layout*/` section:

```
body#index #center_column { width: 980px }[H1]
```

6. Save your `global.css` file.

7. The following screenshot is what you will preview on your front office:

What just happened?

You did some minor editing to the `header.tpl`, `footer.tpl`, and `global.css` file to create the new layout for the main page of your PrestaShop store.

Time for action—Changing the navigation by using third party modules

There are many ways to create a top horizontal bar, which can be linked to various pages in your PrestaShop store. It is much easier to use a third party module, as you can see in the following example:

1. Let's pick one of the top horizontal bars that we can get from the net for free.

2. We shall use one from julienbreux, which can be downloaded for free at `http://www.julien-breux.com/2009/08/25/menu-horizontal-v-1-0/comment-page-3/#comment-3956`.

3. Save this `.tar` file to your computer.

4. Then, upload it to your server through your cPanel or FTP. You should upload it to `/prestashop/modules/`, which is the `modules` directory.

5. Go to your back office and click on the **Modules** tab. You will see the following module:

Julien Breux Developpement - 1 module

Top horizontal menu v1.3
Add a new menu on top of your shop.

Install

6. Enable it by clicking on the **Install** button.

7. You will have to configure it. Click on the **>>Configure** button, and you will be directed to another page.

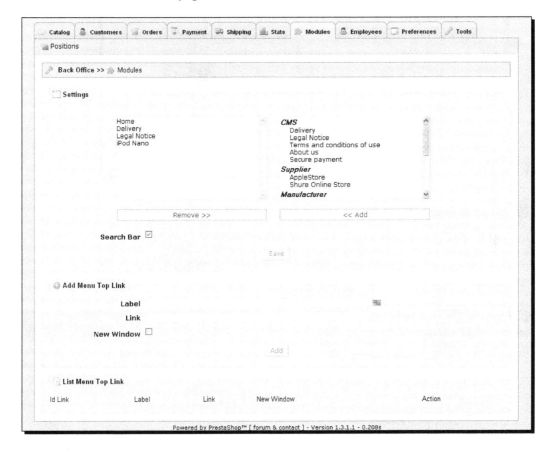

8. On the left column, you will see, by default, a number of items that are already on the top menu bar. You can remove this by clicking on the item you want to remove and then click on **Remove>>**. That particular item will be sent to the right column.

9. The items that are in the right column can be sent to the left column to be added on the top menu bar by doing the same thing. That is, if you want to remove an item from the right column, just click on that item and click on **<<Add**. It will then be moved to the left column.

10. If you want to move a number of items together, just click on the item, then press the *Ctrl* button and click on all the items you want to move. Let's see what you have done in the front office:

What just happened?

You added a top menu bar using an available free module.

However, if the item is not already in the list, you will have to add it. That is what our next task will be.

Time for action—Adding an item on the top menu bar

To add more items on the top menu bar:

1. You will have to do it using the CMS link, which is through our **Back Office | Tools | CMS**; we had covered this in depth in the earlier chapter.

2. Click on **+Add new** and enter the information for the required field.

3. Once completed, click on the **Save** button.

4. Then we can move on to the top menu bar again. Remove the items "iPod" from the left column and add "Contact Us" from the right column to the left.

5. You can also add a new menu top link through the **Add Menu Top Link** feature at the bottom part. Enter the information

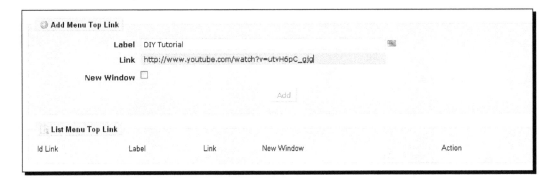

The new label will then be listed at the bottom **List Menu Top Link**, which you can remove later if you want. If it is retained, it will be in the top-right column and ready to be used on the top menu bar as soon as you added it into the left column. Let's move on with this example.

6. To put the product on the top menu bar, you will have to edit the **Catalog** page. As an example, you go to **Back Office | Catalog** and edit the **Categories**.

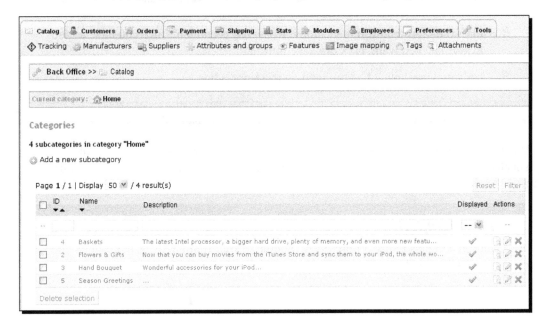

7. All these subcategories will appear automatically in the drop-down list on the **Home** menu. We can also put this on the menu bar by configuring the module. Move the created **Categories** to the left column and they will also appear on the top menu bar.

8. Click the **<<Add** button to include it in the top menu bar. Once you have added everything you want, click the **Save** button.

9. Let's preview how it has changed on the front office.

We will explore more options for you to work on in the next chapter where we will specifically focus on some available free third party modules you can use to make your theming easier.

What just happened?

You explored a means to use a third party module in your theming. This has helped you create a top horizontal menu bar.

Time for action—Omitting some information from the Featured Products block

Based on this layout design, we will modify the **FEATURED PRODUCTS** block. If you want to edit the `homefeatured` **module**, go to `/modules/homefeatured/homefeatured.tpl`.

If you do not want the description on the **FEATURED PRODUCTS** block, you will have to perform the the following steps:

1. Comment the following portion of the `homefeatured.tpl` file. Insert `{*` and `*}` in the starting and at the end of it respectively:

```
<h5><a href="{$product.link}" title="{$product.
name|truncate:32:'...'
   |escape:'htmlall':'UTF-8'}">
   {$product.name|truncate:27:'...'|escape:'htmlall':'UTF-8'}</a>
</h5>
<p class="product_desc"><a href="{$product.
link}" title="{l s='More'm
   od='homefeatured'}">
   {$product.description_short|strip_tags|truncate:130:'...'}</a>
</p>
```

2. The default featured product will then look like the following:

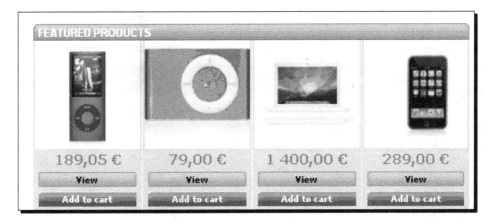

3. You need to edit the following lines to reduce the value to meet your requirements:

```
{assign var='liHeight' value=342}
```

4. Adjust it before you decide on a figure. Then view it in Firebug and adjust the value if required.

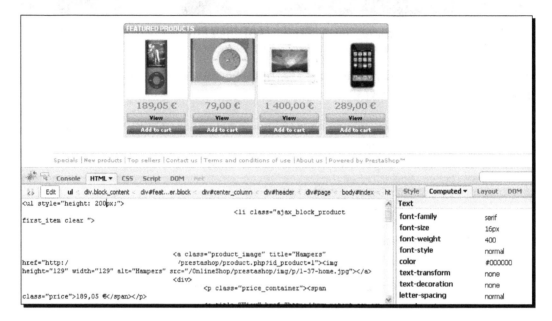

What just happened?

You modified the information to be displayed on the **FEATURED PRODUCTS** block.

Time for action—Replacing the block header tabs and block background images

Our next task is to replace the background images of the modules block. Our theme uses the same sub-pages of the three column. Here we want to replace the background images to different colors to match our gift shop concept.

1. Look in the `img` folders in your PrestaShop directory. The next screenshot shows the theme's `img` folder:

icon	flag_new_bg	thumbs_right
jquery	footer_account	title_bg
address_alias_left	form_bg	title_bg_large
address_alias_right	form-input-bg	
bg_account	header_account	
block_bg	logo_paiement_mastercard	
block_bg_myaccount	logo_paiement_paypal	
block_category_item_bg	logo_paiement_visa	
block_exclusive_bg	onsale_en	
block_exclusive_footer	onsale_es	
block_footer	onsale_fr	
block_footer_myaccount	pagination_bg	
block_header	pagination-bg-current	
block_header_exclusive	pagination-next-border	
block_header_exclusive_cart	pagination-prev-border	
block_header_large	pagination-prevnext-bg	
block_header_myaccount	product-buy-bg	
block_myaccount_header_large	product-short-desc-bg	
block_search_bg	rss	
bullet	sitemap_long	
bullet_alt	sitemap-horizontal	
bullet_myaccount	sitemap-last	
bullet_price	sitemap-top	
button-account	step_current	
button-account-large	step_end	
button-account-mini	step_end_current	
button-account-small	step_standard	
button-large	step_start	
button-large_exclusive	tab_bg	
button-medium	tab_bg_selected	
button-medium_exclusive	tab_bg_selected_short	
button-mini	tab_bg_short	
button-mini_exclusive	table_footer	
button-small	table_header	
button-small_exclusive	thumbs_left	

2. Our next task is to change the following files:

   - `block_header.gif`
   - `block_header_exclusive.gif`
   - `block_header_exclusivecart.gif`
   - `title_bg.gif`

   For the images you want to replace, you can create images with the same format and name.

3. Upload the images to your server to `/themes/mythemes/img/` and overwrite the default images.

Have a go hero—Modifying the module blocks

You can enable all the modules you want to use. In this exercise, install the following module blocks:

- ◆ Newsletter
- ◆ Wish list
- ◆ Specials
- ◆ Cart
- ◆ Top Seller
- ◆ New Products
- ◆ Viewed Products

Position the modules to the appropriate column. We covered positioning modules in depth in *Chapter 2, Customizing PrestaShop Theme Part I*.

Let us go through one example of how to change the `block_header.gif`. Go to your site's cPanel or access your site using FTP. Now, replace all the files we listed and review the changes in the front office.

Time for action—Changing the block content color

Now let's change the background color and the background images of the module blocks. We can review the classes and IDs of the elements using Firebug or a web developer tool (this is also covered in *Chapter 5, Applying Images*).

Let's modify the default block style.

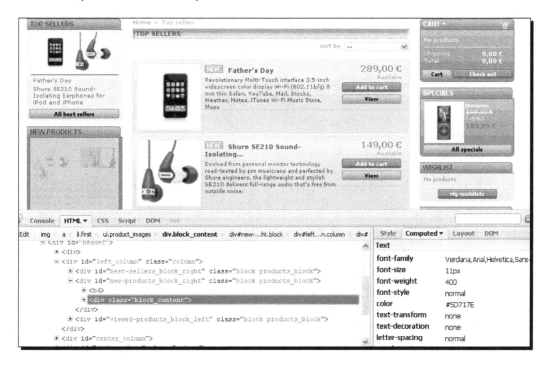

1. You can see the block background color is within
   `<div class ="block_content">`.

2. Look for the following in the `global.css` file:

```
/* Default block style */
div.block {
  margin-bottom: 1em;
  width: 191px
}
#left_column div.block,
 #right_column div.block {
  padding-bottom: 5px;
  background: transparent url('../img/block_footer.gif') no-repeat
  bottom left
}
```

```
div.block h4 {
  text-transform: uppercase;
  font-family: Helvetica, Sans-Serif;
  font-weight: bold;
  font-size: 1.2em;
  padding-left: 0.5em;
  border-bottom: 1px solid #595A5E;
  padding-top: 2px;
  line-height: 1.3em;
  color: #374853;
  height: 19px;
  background: transparent url('../img/block_header.gif') no-repeat
  top left
}
div.block h4 a { color: #374853 }
div.block ul { list-style: none }
div.block ul.tree li { padding-left: 1.2em }
div.block a:hover { text-decoration: underline }
#left_column div.block.block_content a.button_large,
 #right_column div.block .block_content a.button_large { margin: 0
0 0 -3px}
div.block .block_content {
  border-left: 1px #d0d3d8;
  border-right: 1px #d0d3d8;
  padding: 0 0.7em;
  background: #f1f2f4 url('../img/block_bg.jpg') repeat-x bottom
  left;
  min-height: 16px
}
div.block li {
  padding: 0.2em 0 0.2em 0em;
  list-style-position: outside
}
div.block a {
  color: #595a5e;
  text-decoration: none
}
```

3.   Replace the footer of the block by changing the first highlighted item to:

```
#left_column div.block,#right_column div.block {
  padding-bottom: 5px;
  background: #ffcccc
}
```

4. Replace the color of the content by changing the second highlighted item with the same color

```
background: #ffcccc
```

5. Save your changes.

6. Now you have changed the block content.

7. Change the exclusive block background color:

```
/* block exclusive */
#left_column div.exclusive, #right_column div.exclusive {
  background: transparent url('../img/block_exclusive_footer.jpg')
  no-repeat bottom left
}
div.exclusive h4 {
  background: transparent url('../img/block_header_exclusive.gif')
  no-repeat top left;
  color: white
}
div.exclusive h4 a { color: white }
div.exclusive li { margin-top: 0 }
```

```
div.exclusive, div.exclusive a { color: white }
div.exclusive .block_content {
  background: #bdc2c9 url('../img/block_exclusive_bg.jpg')
  repeat-x bottom left;
  border-left: 1px solid #595a5e;
  border-right: 1px solid #595a5e
}
```

8. Change the background color to `#ffcccc`. Insert `background:#ffcccc` where you see the highlighted `background` in the preceding code and omit the rest of that line.

9. Change all the text colors in the exclusive block to `#595a5e` by inserting the code `color: #595a5e` in the highlighted code where you see the property `color`.

10. We will also change the color of the buttons on the **CART**, **WISHLIST**, and **Add to cart** button in the center column.

11. Go to the following section in your `global.css` file.

12. Using Firebug, check the elements and replace them.

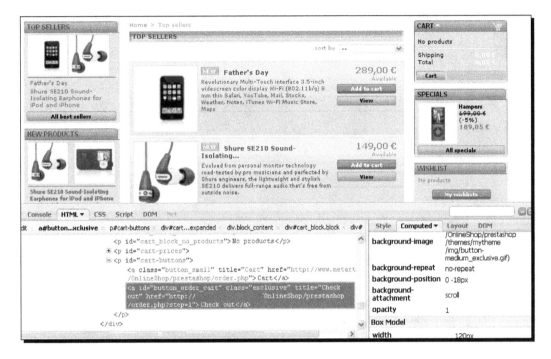

13. From the right column at the bottom, you can see the background image used `/themes/mytheme/img/button-medium_exclusive.gif`

14. The other green buttons, such as **Add to cart** and **My Wishlist**, are also made from `button-medium_exclusive.gif`.

15. Find a good replacement and upload it to your server.

What just happened?

You learned how to change the elements in your theme and you replaced the buttons with different colors and background images.

Validating the theme

It is useful to test code for the theme you just created on various browsers or platforms, as you may note that it may look right on IE but not on Firefox. Try IETester for IE browsers, but this is only for Windows. Find it at `http://www.my-debugbar.com/wiki/IETester/HomePage`

Some of the best sites to use for validating are `www.validator.w3.org/` and `http://xhtml-css.com/`.

If you have been using PrestaShop 1.3.1 for development work, always test it on the other version to see compatibility. This will be useful for those who want to use your theme. More on validating in *Chapter 8, Deploying Your New Themes*.

Packaging the new theme

Packaging your own unique theme for PrestaShop can involve slightly more than just letting your new theme be installed and run automatically, the same way as you created it.

When you want to package your theme, consider having a step-by-step readme file for anyone wanting to use your theme.

If you have made the theme on your local computer, you will need to `zip` the file and upload it to the PrestaShop site you want to use it on.

When your theme is ready, you must place a file representing the theme called `preview.jpg` in the theme's root folder (for example, `../themes/mytheme`). This file must be a 100x100 pixels `.jpg` file. More detail on this is discussed in *Chapter 8, Deploying Your New Themes*.

In the previous version of PrestaShop v1.2.5.0, it was possible to change the name and description in `themes/mytheme/config/conf.xml`. However, the `config` folder was deleted in PrestaShop v1.3.

It is not possible to define the theme name, version, author, and description in PrestaShop, except by means of commenting in the file.

Making a two column theme

Our second mission is to change the layout from three to two columns with adjustments to your pages.

Now imagine your aim is to have a two column webpage throughout your PrestaShop store, instead of three as in the default theme.

Just `{* comment *}` the following code in `header.tpl` to remove the left column:

```
<!-- Left -->

<div id="left_column" class="column">

    {$HOOK_LEFT_COLUMN}

</div>
```

Or comment the following code in `footer.tpl` to remove the right column:

```
<!-- Right -->
<div id="right_column" class="column">
    {$HOOK_RIGHT_COLUMN}
</div>
```

Then increase the width of the `#center_column` in `global.css` to fill up the space of the missing column.

Get Smarty

You may not be familiar with what Smarty is. But Smarty is really an old familiar friend we know from PHP. It is a web template system written in PHP.

Smarty separates PHP code (often represented as business logic) from HTML (often represented as presentation logic).

Smarty is known as a "Template Engine". However, a more accurate description would be that it acts as a "Template/Presentation Framework."

It provides the programmer and template designer with a wealth of tools to automate tasks commonly dealt with at the presentation layer of an application.

It must be emphasized as to what it does as a Framework to template because Smarty is not a simple tag-replacing template engine.

It is possible to use Smarty for such a simple purpose, but its main focus is on quick and easy development and deployment of an application, while maintaining high-performance, scalability, security, and potential for future growth.

More information on Smarty can be found at `www.smarty.net`

Knowing jQuery

You may have come across something like the following in a PrestaShop file:

```
$("p.neat").addClass("ohmy").show("slow");
```

This is how jQuery code looks. jQuery is basically a JavaScript library that allows easier and faster web development through simplifying Java scripting and AJAX programming.

The code is located in the `js` folder in the specific theme directory. JavaScripts are more often used as add on modules.

You may get better acquainted with jQuery at the following sites:

```
http://docs.jquery.com/Tutorials:How_jQuery_
Works#jQuery:_The_Basics
http://jqueryui.com/
http://jquery.org/
http://www.learningjquery.com/
```

Summary

In this chapter, we worked through the entire process of creating a new theme for your PrestaShop site. In fact, there are many more things you can do to make your site unique once you get the grasp of how things are done.

In summary, we have covered:

- Some theory about PrestaShop architecture and philosophy
- A practical step-by-step approach for making a new theme for a PrestaShop site
- Ideas for creating the raw elements, modifying the relevant files, and enabling the required modules to combine into a new look for the site
- Validation of your theme
- Additional knowhow that will help you become an expert in theming.

You can apply this knowledge to other aspects of your PrestaShop theming. You can try to change some other elements that have not been covered, such as the icons or the buttons, by using the web developer tools to identify the elements and replace the elements with your own creations. You will also find that a number of third party modules can be useful to save you from doing a lot of code editing. There are other simple ways through other minor code editing to make your theming easier.

We will learn some of these means, such as using some third party modules and making minor changes to the code to make your theming easier, in the next chapter.

7

Tips and Tricks to Make PrestaShop Theming Easier

You must have realized by now that creating a new theme with PrestaShop is fun. Editing the theme becomes a simple chore as PrestaShop uses a CSS-based layout.

Adding some interesting stuff into your website will make it more attractive and meaningful for site users to return.

This chapter explores tips and tricks on how to make it easier to develop themes. It also explains ways to use some additional interactivity through the use of third party modules and JavaScript, which can add zest to your new online store.

Firstly, we will look into adding interactive elements within various sections such as the center column blocks (editorial and featured blocks), modifying the navigation element (like moving the manufacturer block link to the top menu bar), and spreading the categories from the categories blocks at the top menu buttons.

Most of these actions will require the use of some third party modules, which you can download easily from the various links we mention here. However, in case the links change in the future, we have also appended the files that you can re-compile and load to your site, if required.

Adding more interactivity to your PrestaShop site

A static looking site can be quite boring, especially if you are running a website trying to sell stuff online. It is much more difficult to create a buzz when compared to the brick-and-mortar shop, where visitors see other users browsing the shop and buying in a busy store with loud punchy music; which can increase their adrenalin and encourage them to to buy more.

How can an online store be made more interactive and dynamic, so that it gets more conversion from visitors to purchasers?

Adding the right interactivity can add visual interest and attract users. There are a number of ways that you can add to your new site to make it visually pleasing and suit the theme you are creating.

Now look at the following section (where the home page logo is displayed by default) and consider what you want to replace it with.

We could choose to add some video perhaps or a slideshow of some top products or just a flash `swf` file.

How do we do that now?

Time for action—Adding YouTube or other video element

Now, there are plenty of "add YouTube" modules for PrestaShop on the net. As they are mostly free modules, you will need to read some reviews or test them before actually using any of them.

The one that I have used here was obtained from the PrestaShop forum, but the link to the demo is missing.

1. You can download the `zip` file of the YouTube module at: `http://www. PrestaShop.com/forums/viewthread/10352`

In case you cannot find it, I will just explain the module a bit.

These files are basically similar to the editorial module you have on your default PrestaShop. There are three key files in the default editorial module, which are `editorial.php`, `editorial.xml`, and `editorial.tpl`.

For the YouTube module, the names are slightly different. The file is named as **editorialyoutube.tpl**. You can see the files that you will find in the **editorialyoutube** module in the following screenshot:

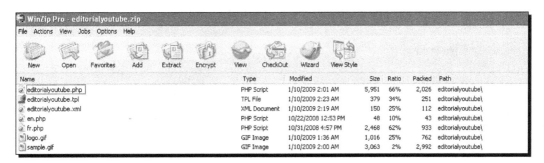

2. Once downloaded, you may either use it on your localhost or upload it to your server in the modules directory (for example, `/prestashop/modules`).

3. Unzip the file into the `modules` directory, and you will get the `editorialyoutube` folder.

Time for action—Installing and enabling the YouTube module

Now, let's go back to your back office administration panel

1. Click the **Module** tab, and you will see the new module which is already shown on the screen. Go to **Back Office** | **Modules** | and scroll down to the **Tools** list.

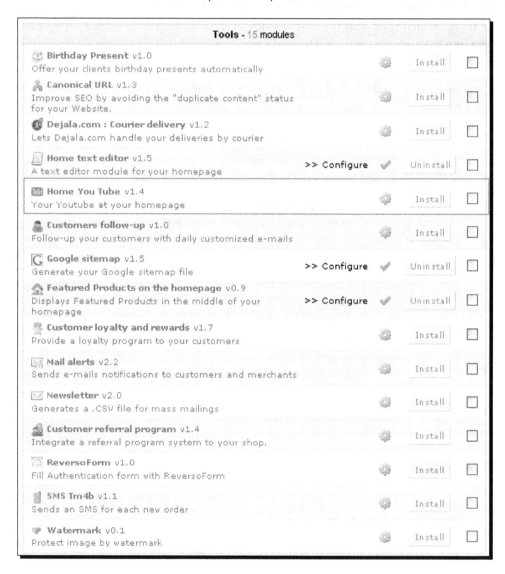

2. You will have to install and enable the `editorialyoutube` module. The way to install and enable is the same as any other default module's installation, as we have learned in the previous chapter.

3. You should see the following, once you clicked the installation button.

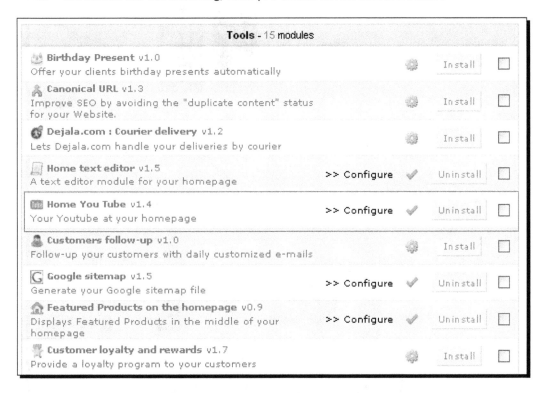

4. We can configure the YouTube module later after we position the module in the front office.

5. Let's go to the front office and have a look at where it is positioned.

Time for action—Positioning the YouTube module

By default, when you installed and enabled the module, the home YouTube video will be displayed at the bottom of the center column of your front page.

So you will need to move it up to the top of the center column to make it appear in the home page logo position. Now, let's position it accordingly by executing the following steps:

1. Click on the **Position** button within your administration's **Module** tab (Go to **Back Office | Modules |** and click on **Positions**).

2. Scroll and find the **Homepage content**.

3. Click on the **Home You Tube** module, and drag it to the position you want to move it to, for example, to the top, as shown in the following screenshot:

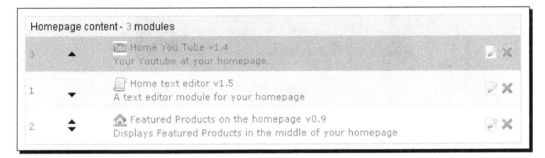

4. After doing this, you may want to delete the **Home text editor** module by removing it from the hook, if you prefer. This will be displayed only on the **FEATURED PRODUCTS** block and the **Home You Tube** in the center column.

5. Now, let's preview it to see how it looks on your front office:

What just happened?

You have just installed, enabled, and positioned the YouTube module in your PrestaShop site.

Time for action—Configuring the YouTube module

With regards to the content of the video you want to display, you will have to configure the video link you want to display.

1. Go back to the **Back Office | Modules** tab, and click on **>>Configure** for your **Home You Tube** module.

You will be taken to the following page:

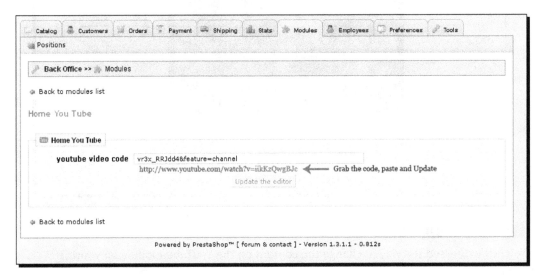

2. You need to check the code on the YouTube website. It is the code that appears in your browser bar when you view a video from the YouTube site.

3. Insert the code into the field for **youtube video code**.

4. Click on the **Update the editor** button.

Have a look at the result now in the following screenshot:

What just happened?

You just witnessed the way to change the content on the YouTube module on your home page.

Time for action—Setting the player for the YouTube module

By default, the module is on autoplay.

1. If you prefer to change the setting so that the video plays only when it is clicked, you will have to go to the `modules` folder and open the `editorialyoutube.tpl`.

```
<!-- Module Editorial -->
  <div id="editorial_block_center" class="editorial_block"
  align="center">
    <embed src="http://www.youtube.com/v/{if $xml->body->$title}
    {$xml->body-
    >$title|stripslashes}{/if}&autoplay=1&hl=en&fs=1"
    type="application/x- shockwave-flash"
    allowscriptaccess="always" allowfullscreen="true"
    width="540" height="437"></embed>
  </div>
<!-- /Module Editorial -->
```

2. Look for `&autoplay=1`, and change it to read `&autoplay=0`.

3. Save the file.

What just happened?

By changing this setting, the user will be required to click on the play button to start instead of the YouTube video being automatically playing once the page loads.

Instead of using YouTube, you may also use other video sharing website such as Dailymotion, where the free module is available from the same thread.

Video contents can be engaging, but for store purposes, make sure it suits your store concept. You may use some existing YouTube reels or make up a few of your own, post them on a channel on YouTube, and load them on your store as we just learned.

Pop Quiz

1. Where do you upload the third party module in your server?

   a. `/modules`

   b. `/tools`

   c. `/prestashop/`

2. Based on our exercise, how do you configure the modules in the Back Office?

   a. Go to **Back Office** | **Modules** | **Blocks**

   b. Go to **Back Office** | **Modules** | **Tools**

   c. Go to **Back Office** | **Tools**

Adding carousels in your PrestaShop site

Another way to make your theme more interesting while relating the elements to display your store products is by using a slideshow in place of the video.

A carousel (from French *carrousel*, and Italian *carosello*), or merry-go-round, consists of a rotating circular platform for the "riders".

Briefly, the jcarousel that we are using is based on this carousel concept where items are rotated using a platform. This jcarousel is a jQuery plug-in that can be used to display a list of items in a horizontal or vertical order. These items can be static HTML content or loaded with (or without) AJAX. The carousel can be scrolled back and forth (with or without animation). It doesn't really rotate circularly, but gives the impression that it does.

jQuery is described as a fast and concise JavaScript library that simplifies HTML document traversing, event handling, animating, and AJAX interactions for rapid web development. jQuery is designed to change the way JavaScript is written.

Concept aside, we will work on what is there to be used within the carousel.

Time for action—Using the jQuery carousel

The jQuery carousel will loop infinitely over the items when the next or the previous button is clicked. Generally, this module can be created on your own.

However, there are some readymade jcarousel modules that you may download from the various PrestaShop sites.

1. Download jcarousel.zip, and save it on your hard disk. You may download it from http://www.PrestaShop.com/forums/viewthread/19951.

    If this link is unavailable, you can get it from the appended code bundle.

2. Upload the zip file to your server or if you are using a development site, place it in the correct folder on your localhost. Make sure you locate it to the modules directory. (/modules/)

3. Then, extract jcarousel.zip and copy the jcarousel folder to your shop's modules directory. You can find slides and assets folders inside the jcarousel folder, as shown in the following screenshot:

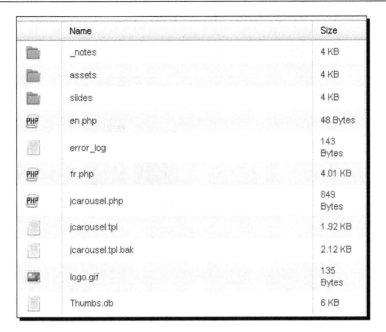

4. Go to the **Back Office | Modules** tab. Here you can find **jcarousel module** inside the **Home** section.

5. Click on the **Install** button and you will have enabled it.

You should see the following screen in your front office browser.

Time for action—Positioning the jcarousel within the home page

You may want to move the `jcarousel` slideshow to the top position or to another position within the home page. The steps to do so are as follows:

1. Go to **Back Office | Modules |** and click on the **Positions** tab. By default, once you have enabled the module, it is hooked at **Homepage content**. You should have this in your **Homepage content** hook as follows:

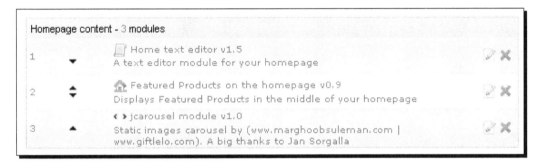

2. The way to move it to the top is by clicking on the module near the arrow, and when you see a four headed arrow as the cursor, drag it to your desired position. There is no need to save this, as the position you moved to is what will appear on the front office.

3. Once you have moved it to the correct position, preview it in your front office browser.

What just happened?

You learned how to install and enable the `jcarousel` in your home page. You also now know how to position it within the home page.

Have a go hero—Replacing images in the jcarousel

Unfortunately, at this point of time, we do not have a back office configuration on this module to replace the images in the slideshow. The images loaded in the slideshows are located in the `/modules/jcarousel/slides` folder.

In order to replace the images shown on the slideshow, you will have to edit the file within the `jcarousel` module folder, which is `jcarousel.tpl`. You will have to replace the image path according to your image file and link paths.

1. The following is the part within the `jcarousel.tpl` file that you need to change, according to what image you want to add and which product or manufacturer page you want to link to:

```
<li><a href="manufacturer.php?id_manufacturer=3"><img
  src="{$module_dir}slides/Slide1.jpg" alt="" width="533"
  height="260" border="0" /></a>
</li>
<li><a href="manufacturer.php?id_manufacturer=3"><img
  src="{$module_dir}slides/Slide2.jpg" alt="" width="533"
  height="260" border="0" /></a>
</li>
<li><a href="product.php?id_product=17"><img
  src="{$module_dir}slides/Slide3.jpg" width="533" height="260"
  alt="" /></a>
</li>
<li><a href="product.php?id_product=14"><img
  src="{$module_dir}slides/Slide4.jpg" alt="" width="533"
  height="260" border="0" /></a>
</li>
<li><a href="manufacturer.php?id_manufacturer=3"><img
  src="{$module_dir}slides/Slide7.jpg" alt="" width="533"
  height="260" border="0" /></a>
</li>
<li><a href="product.php?id_product=26"><img
  src="{$module_dir}slides/Slide5.jpg" width="533" height="260"
  alt="" /></a>
</li>
<li><a href="product.php?id_product=17"><img
  src="{$module_dir}slides/Slide6.jpg" alt="" width="533"
  height="260" border="0" /></a>
</li>
```

2. Go to your front office and review the image paths of the items you want to link or feature in this slideshow.

For example, if you want to feature the iPod, first find the link to the page, as shown in the following screenshot:

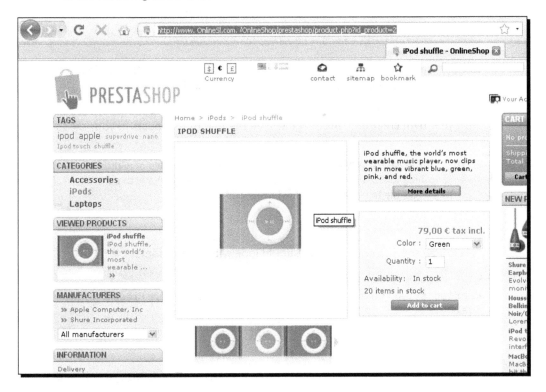

3. The page you want the slideshow image to link to is as indicated on the browser. For example, if you want the iPod shuffle page to be featured, you will have to insert the correct link in the `tpl` file.

4. This is an example of how the image link `<a href>` should be replaced with:
   `http://www.yourdomain.com/prestashop/product.php?id_product=2`

5. Replace the original link with your own link, as follows:

```
<li><a href=http://www.yourdomain.com/prestashop/product.
php?id_product=2><img src="{$module_dir}slides/Slide2.jpg" alt=""
width="533" height="260" border="0" /></a></li>
```

6. Replace the image filename based on what you have replaced within the slides folder.

```
<li><a href=http://www.yourdomain.com/prestashop/product.
php?id_product=2><img src="{$module_dir}slides/Slide2.jpg" alt=""
width="533" height="260" border="0" /></a></li>
```

7. Just add on more of these lines within the `tpl` file and delete the original as you do it, according to the amount of images you want to add.

8. Go to the `slides` folder. Replace the slides (`Slide1.jpg`, `Slide2.jpg`, and so on) with your own creation. This image will be the one that appears in your slideshow.

> The easiest way to do this is to use the same size image of width 533, height 260, and the format `jpg`. Otherwise, you will have to edit the `tpl` file to match the image format and name.

9. Save the file you have changed.

This is how the `jcarousel.tpl` should look within your domain.

```
<!-- MODULE jcarousel -->
<script type="text/javascript" src="{$module_dir}assets/jquery.
jcarousel.pack.js"></script>
<!--
  jCarousel core stylesheet
-->
<link rel="stylesheet" type="text/css"href="{$module_dir}assets/
jquery.jcarousel.css" />
<!--
  jCarousel skin stylesheet
-->
<link rel="stylesheet" type="text/css" href="{$module_dir}assets/
skin.css" />
<script type="text/javascript" src="{$module_dir}assets/carousel_
start.js">
</script>
<div id="mycarouselHolder" align="center" style="padding:0 0 10px
  0;height:260px;overflow: hidden; clear:both">
<div id="wrap">
  <ul id="mycarousel" class="jcarousel-skin-tango">
```

```
        <li><a href="http://www.yourdomain.com/product.php?id_
product=2"><img src="{$module_dir}slides/Slide1.jpg" alt=""
width="533" height="260" vspace="0" border="0" /></a></li>
        <li><a href="http://www.yourdomain.com/manufacturer.php?id_
manufacturer=3"><img src="{$module_dir}slides/Slide2.jpg" alt=""
width="533" height="260" vspace="0" border="0" /></a></li>
        <li><a href="http://www.yourdomain.com/product.php?id_
product=17"><img src="{$module_dir}slides/Slide3.jpg" alt=""
width="533" height="260" vspace="0" border="0" /></a></li>
        <li><a href="http://www.yourdomain.com/product.php?id_
product=14"><img src="{$module_dir}slides/Slide4.jpg" alt=""
width="533" height="260" vspace="0" border="0" /></a></li>
        <li><a href="http://www.yourdomain.com/manufacturer.php?id_
manufacturer=15"><img src="{$module_dir}slides/Slide5.jpg" alt=""
width="533" height="260" vspace="0" border="0" /></a></li>
        <li><a href="http://www.yourdomain.com/product.php?id_
product=26"><img src="{$module_dir}slides/Slide6.jpg" alt=""
width="533" height="260" vspace="0" border="0" /></a></li>
        <li><a href="http://www.yourdomain.com/product.php?id_
product=17"><img src="{$module_dir}slides/Slide7.jpg" alt=""
width="533" height="260" vspace="0" border="0" /></a></li>
    </ul>
 </div>
 </div>
 <!-- /MODULE jcarousel -->
```

10. Preview it in your front office browser.

Time for action—Changing the attributes

You may want to change some of the attributes of the carousel, for example, expanding the size of the box and so on.

It is possible to directly edit the `jcarousel.tpl` file. It is much easier to edit the CSS file, so the changes can be affected in one go.

1. Go to `modules/jcarousel/assets/skin.css`.

   If you are not sure how to go about it, open your Firebug and review the element.

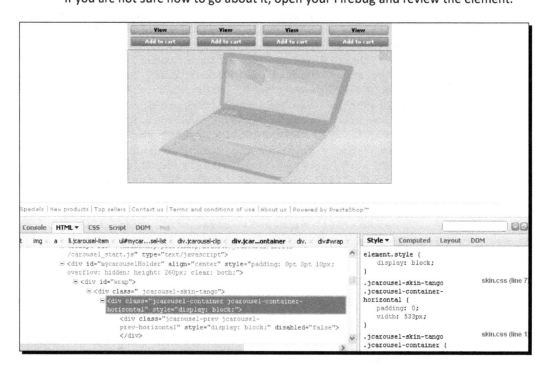

2. Modify the width and height to your liking to suit your new theme. The following is a portion of the `skin.css` file, which you will have to change according to the modifications you made to the previous file.

```
.jcarousel-skin-tango .jcarousel-container {
  background: #F0F6F9;
  border: 1px solid #c3c3c3;
  padding:0;
}
.jcarousel-skin-tango .jcarousel-container-horizontal {
  width: 533px;
  padding: 0;
}
.jcarousel-skin-tango .jcarousel-container-vertical {
   width: 533px;
  height: 260px;
  padding: 0;
}
```

3. Change the size according to what you want.

4. Save the changes.

5. Preview it in your browser.

 If you enjoyed using carousels and would like to explore and dig further on this, refer to http://api.jquery.com/animate/ and http://sorgalla.com/projects/jcarousel/

Limitation

Generally, you can't use different JavaScript libraries together on the same page. For example, do not use Moo Tools in combination with jQuery. The jcarousel uses jQuery and therefore will not work with any other JavaScript modules.

Gallery view

Another module that you can use in your center column can be the gallery view.

This module can be downloaded at: `http://www.PrestaShop.com/forums/viewthread/26127/P0/third_party_modules/modulegalleryview2_dot_0`

Time for action—Adding gallery view

1. Download the file and save it to your hard disk.

2. Then upload it to your modules directory in your server or put it in the modules directory in your localhost.

3. Extract the file.

4. Go to your back office. Install and enable the module.

5. Go to **Position**, and check if it is hooked to the right section of your page.

6. Move the module up or down the hook as you wish, depending on what you want on top within the center column of your home page.

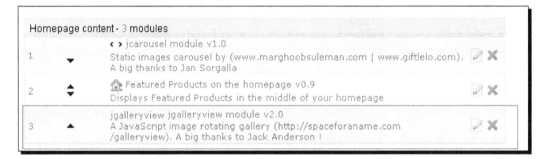

7. You may delete one of the slideshows and move the gallery to the top to replace the `jcarousel`.

Time for action—Replacing images in the gallery

In order to change your images, you will need to edit the `jgalleryview.tpl` file and replace the images in the `modules/slides` folder.

1. Let's look up the `jgalleryview.tpl` file:

```
<!-- MODULE jGalleryview -->
<script type="text/javascript" src="{$module_dir}assets/jquery.galleryview-2.0-pack.js"></script>
<script type="text/javascript" src="{$module_dir}assets/jquery.easing.1.3.js"></script>
```

```
<script type="text/javascript" src="{$module_dir}assets/jquery.
timers-1.1.2.js"></script>
<!--
   jGalleryview core stylesheet
-->
<link rel="stylesheet" type="text/css" href="{$module_dir}assets/
galleryview.css" />
<!--
   jGalleryview template
-->
<script type="text/javascript" src="{$module_dir}assets/
galleryview_start.js"></script>
<div id="galleryviewHolder" align="center" style="padding:0 0 10px
0;overflow: hidden; clear:both">
<div id="wrap">
<ul id=gallery>
<li><span class=panel-overlay>this is an overlay</span>
<img src="{$module_dir}slides/01.jpg">
<li><span class=panel-overlay>this is another overlay</span>
<img src="{$module_dir}slides/02.jpg">
<li><span class=panel-overlay>this is yet another overlay</span>
<img src="{$module_dir}slides/03.jpg">
<li><span class=panel-overlay>this is an overlay too</span>
<img src="{$module_dir}slides/04.jpg">
<li><span class=panel-overlay>this is an overlay</span>
<img src="{$module_dir}slides/05.jpg">
<li><span class=panel-overlay>this is another overlay</span>
<img src="{$module_dir}slides/06.jpg">
<li><span class=panel-overlay>this is yet another overlay</span>
<img src="{$module_dir}slides/07.jpg">
<li><span class=panel-overlay>this is an overlay too</span>
<img src="{$module_dir}slides/08.jpg">
</ul>
</div>
</div>
<!-- /MODULE jGalleryview -->
```

2. Notice the lists of `jpg` files within the code. These are the files you need to replace in the slides folder.

3. Go to `/jgalleryview/jgalleryview/slides`. this is where the images displayed are located in the module.

4. Upload or put your images in the slides directory. The highlighted image filenames are the files you need to replace. You can do that either by using the same naming conventions for your image files or replace the filename with your own image filenames, for example, replace `04.jpg` with `myimage.jpg` or `myimage.gif`.

5. If you made any changes to the `jgalleryview.tpl`, you will need to save it.

6. Preview it in the front office.

Have a go hero—Modifying the jgalleryview module dimension

You can also customize the dimension of the gallery viewer.

To change the size of this block, perform the following steps:

1. Go to asset directory and look up `galleryview_start.js`.

2. Look up the `panel_width` and `panel_height` in `galleryview_start.js`.

3. Say, if you would like to have a larger image to fill up the center column, you may want to widen the panel, but you will need to make some adjustments.

```
$(document).ready(function(){
    $('#gallery').galleryView({
      panel_width: 500,
      panel_height: 188,
      frame_width: 100,
      frame_height: 100,
      transition_speed: 350,
      easing: 'easeInOutQuad'
    });
});
```

You may also change the easing options by replacing it with swing or another mode of easing.

 Check out `http://gsgd.co.uk/sandbox/jquery/easing/` to consider a number of options for your animation.

Adding interactivity in the Featured Products block

Similar to the manner in which we created the interactivity on the home page logo position, we will learn how to add some interaction on the **Featured Products block** of the store.

Time for action—Adding a moving box in the Featured Products block

Another module that is quite interesting that you may use in the **Featured Products block** is available at `http://www.ecartservice.net/03082009/moving-boxes-home-featured-jquery-module/`

This module is also based on `jQuery` and features the products in moving boxes.

The moving box interacts with the click of the arrow button on the sides. It will show the next featured product once you click this arrow (previous and next are converted into red arrow buttons).

It can replace your default theme, which displays four featured items in the featured blocks in the center column. This moving box enhances the interactivity and looks quite cool too.

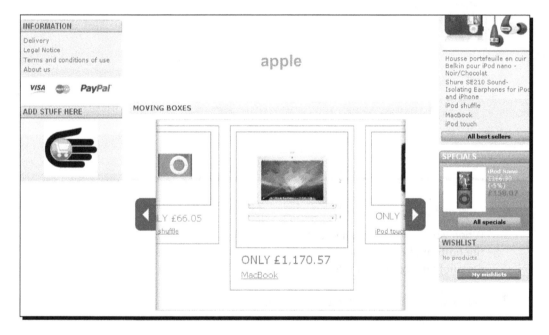

1. Download the file from the mentioned link. Save it in your computer.

2. Upload it in the `modules` file to your server.

3. Unzip it and you will see a new folder containing all the files.

4. Go to your back office panel, and click on the **Modules** tab.

You should be able to see it in the modules list. Install and enable this module.

5. You can then configure the setting. Adjust the maximum display of the products to be shown on your new featured block.

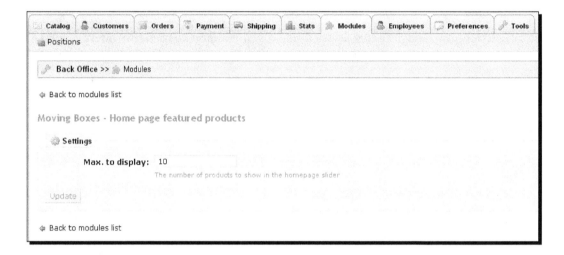

6. Click on the **Update** button.

When you view it through your front office, you will notice that it is, by default, at the bottom of the default **Featured Products** module block. You may delete this default featured block in the **Positions** tab.

7. Go to **Back Office** | **Modules** | **Positions**.

You will note that the **Moving Boxes** module is hooked (by default, once installed) at the **Header of pages** and the **Homepage content** (the home hook).

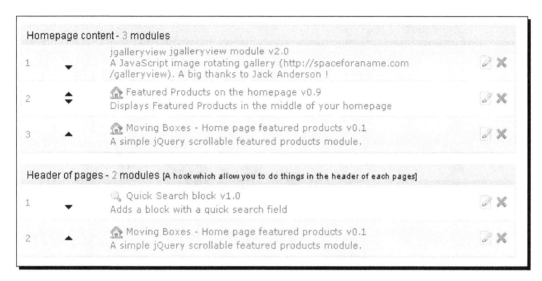

You need to leave it hooked to both, if it is to be displayed correctly.

8. Now, you can delete the **Featured Products** block from this home page position. Just click on the close icon (on the extreme right side), and we will have the moving boxes replacing it at its (the **Featured Products** block) default position.

Using top navigation menu bar

Other than modifying the center column, you may want to change the way you organize the default blocks in the menu bar (manufacturers, best prices, top seller, and so on). Instead of having it on separate blocks, you may want to have some or all of them in a horizontal menu bar at the top section of the home page.

There is no need to tweak the files to do this, it can be be done quite simply by adding a third party module.

Time for action—Adding a horizontal menu

The original discussion about this can be viewed at `http://www.PrestaShop.com/forums/viewthread/17546`

The block highlighted by red outline in the preceding screenshot is what we want to achieve in our next task.

1. Download the module from the link and save it to your hard disk.

2. Upload the `zip` file to your `/prestashop/modules` directory in your server and extract the content.

3. You will need to edit two files, as it is important for hook activation. The first file `header.php`, can be found in the `modules` directory.

4. Open your `header.php` file and edit the following:

```
$smarty->assign(array(
  'HOOK_HEADER' => Module::hookExec('header'),
  'HOOK_LEFT_COLUMN' => Module::hookExec('leftColumn'),
  'HOOK_TOP' => Module::hookExec('top'),
  'static_token' => Tools::getToken(false),
  'token' => Tools::getToken(),
  'priceDisplayPrecision' => _PS_PRICE_DISPLAY_PRECISION_,
  'content_only' => intval(Tools::getValue('content_only'))
));
```

5. Edit it to the following:

```
$smarty->assign(array(
  'HOOK_HEADER' => Module::hookExec('header'),
  'HOOK_LEFT_COLUMN' => Module::hookExec('leftColumn'),
  'HOOK_WIZNAV' => Module::hookExec('wiznav'),
  'HOOK_TOP' => Module::hookExec('top'),
  'static_token' => Tools::getToken(false),
  'token' => Tools::getToken(),
  'priceDisplayPrecision' => _PS_PRICE_DISPLAY_PRECISION_,
  'content_only' => intval(Tools::getValue('content_only'))
));
```

6. Look up your particular theme directory for the second file, that is, `header.tpl` (say: `/PrestaShop/themes/theme1/header.tpl`).

7. Now add the following code to this theme file (`header.tpl`)

```
<div>
  {$HOOK_WIZNAV}
</div>
```

8. This is how it ends up:

```
<div>
    <h1 id="logo"><a href="{$base_dir}"
    title="{$shop_name|escape:'htmlall':'UTF-8'}"><img
    src="{$img_ps_dir}logo.jpg" alt="{$shop_name|escape:'htmlall':
    'UTF-8'}" /></a></h1>
  <div id="header">
    {$HOOK_TOP}
  </div>
      <div>
        {$HOOK_WIZNAV}
      </div>
</div>
```

The highlighted lines are the inserted code.

9. Next, go to the back office **Modules** tab where you will see the **Wiznav** module already parked but in an uninstalled state.

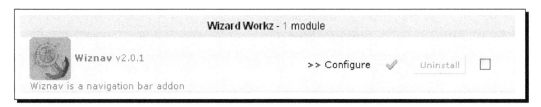

10. Similarly, install and enable the module by clicking on the **Install** button.

11. Click on the **>>Configure** button. You will be taken to the following page.

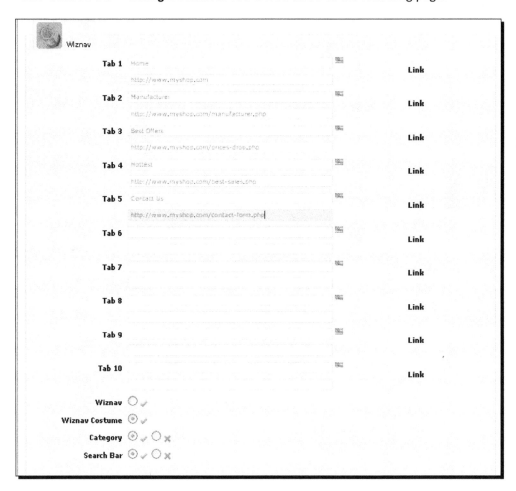

If you have **Category** and **Search Bar** in the menu, enable the radio button next to them. Then change the example domain name to your own.

12. Click on the **Save** button.

Time for action—Using multiple languages on the Wiznav top navigation bar module

If you are using multiple languages on your site, you will need to translate all the tabs to the respective languages.

1. Go to **Back Office** | **Tools** | **Translations**.

2. Choose **Modules Translations**

3. Click on the flag according to the language to be translated in.

4. Search for the **PrestaShop – wiznav – 31 expressions**.

This is very important, especially if you are using the Wiznav custom bar with the **Category** and **Search** tab set to ON. If you don't do it, the **Category** and **Search** tab won't show as they should.

What just happened?

You just explored an easy way to create a theme using a top navigation bar.

Limitations

The languages included are English, French, and Spanish. You are required to translate if you are using another language which is not included in the package.

Time for action—Changing the color and text of the menu bar

You may want to have a different background color on the module bar.

1. Go to the `img` folder in the modules directory (`wiznav/img`).

2. Edit or replace the following images:
- `blank.gif`
- `blank_over.gif`
- `blank_overa.gif`
- `blanka.gif`
- `blankbg.gif`

3. The default color is of a bluish tone. So replace it if you prefer.

Another way to change the look of the menu bar is to change the text color.

1. To change the color of the text, open the `wiznav.css` file at `wiznav/css/wiznav.css`.

2. Look for the following items that you may want change. For example, text color, font type, and size.

```
#nav li a.top_link {display:block; float:left; height:36px; line-height:27px; color:#ccc; text-decoration:none; font-size:13px; font-weight:bold; padding:0 0 0 6px; cursor:pointer;background: url(../img/blank.gif);}
```

3. Edit them according to the following block of code:

```
#nav li.top_blank a.top_blank
{display:block; float:left; height:36px; line-height:27px; color:#ccc; text-decoration:none; font-size:14px; font-weight:bold; padding:0 0 0 0px; cursor:pointer;background: url(../img/blankbg.gif);}
```

4. Save the file.

5. Upload it again to overwrite your existing file, or if you edited on your server, save the file.

6. Preview the changes in your front office.

Time for action—Putting Categories in the horizontal top menu

In the default PrestaShop theme, the categories are listed in a **CATEGORIES** block. We have just learned how to have a link for categories in the top horizontal menu using the Wiznav module

Some would prefer a theme that will straight away show all the categories that we have in our store in a top menu where all the categories are displayed automatically as horizontal menus.

The next module used can simplify theming. It is the one that displays all the categories within the default categories block, spread into the top menu.

You may find the original discussion at: `http://www.PrestaShop.com/forums/viewthread/26478`.

1. Download the module, which is referred to as **blockcategoriestopsc 1.2**.

2. Install and enable the module.

3. If you already have a horizontal top menu, as we discussed earlier, it will appear on top of it.

4. You need to set the width through the configuration page.

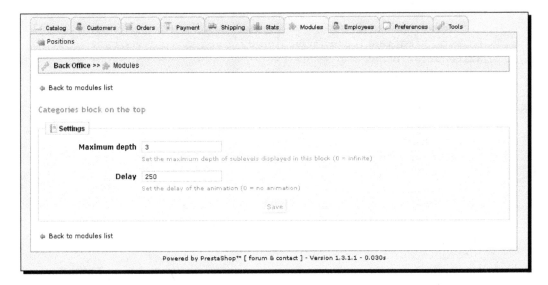

5. You will get the following:

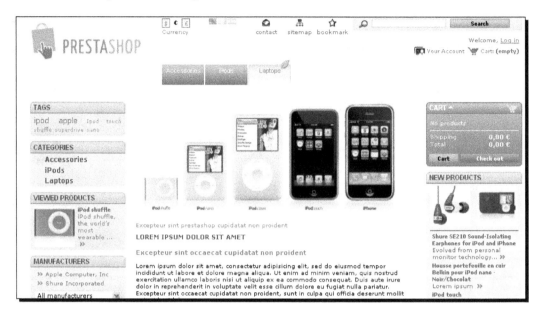

6. You will need to edit the `droppy.css` file to change the color or any other attributes. The highlighted code is the background color that you need to modify if you want to change the color.

```
/* Essentiels - configurer ce qui suit */
/* enrichissement menu, position */
#categories_block_top_sc_ul {
  background-color: transparent;
  text-align: center;
  top: 8px;
}
/* enrichissement sous-menu */
#categories_block_top_sc_ul ul {
  border-bottom: 1px solid #5D717E;
  top: 48px;
}
/* enrichissement 2 ème niveau sous-menu */
#categories_block_top_sc_ul ul ul{
  border-top: 1px solid #5D717E;
}
/* enrichissement catégories */
#categories_block_top_sc_ul a {
  background: url('../img/menu_on.gif') no-repeat;
```

```css
  font-family: Arial;
  color: white;
  font-size: 12px;
  width:84px;
  height: 48px;
  padding: 13px 1px;
  text-decoration:none;
}
#categories_block_top_sc_ul a.selected {
  background: url('../img/menu_over.gif') no-repeat;
  color: black;
}
#categories_block_top_sc_ul a.hover {
  background: url('../img/menu_over.gif') no-repeat;
  color: #5D717E;
}
/* enrichissement sous-catégories */
#categories_block_top_sc_ul ul li a {
  background: white;
  border-right: 1px solid #5D717E;
  border-left: 1px solid #5D717E;
  height:20px;
  width:145px;
  color: #5D717E;
  font-size: 12px;
  font-weight:normal;
  text-indent: 10px;
  text-align: left;
  padding-top: 2px;
  padding-bottom: 2px;
  text-decoration:none;
  line-height:20px;
}
#categories_block_top_sc_ul ul a {
  margin-top: 0px;
  /* opacity: 0.9; */
  /* filter: alpha(opacity=90); */
  border-bottom: none;
}
#categories_block_top_sc_ul ul a.hover {
  background: #B1C903;
  color: white;
}
```

```css
#categories_block_top_sc_ul ul a.selected{
  background: #B1C903;
  color: white;
}
/* enrichissement 2ème niveau sous-catégories */
#categories_block_top_sc_ul ul ul li a {
  background: #F3F7D9;
  height:20px;
  width:145px;
  color: #5D717E;
  font-size: 12px;
  font-weight:normal;
  text-indent: 10px;
  text-align: left;
  padding-top: 2px;
  padding-bottom: 2px;
  text-decoration:none;
  line-height:20px;
}
#categories_block_top_sc_ul ul ul a {
  margin-top: 0px;
  /* opacity: 0.9; */
  /* filter: alpha(opacity=90); */
}
#categories_block_top_sc_ul ul ul a.hover {
  background: #B1C903;
  color: white;
}
#categories_block_top_sc_ul ul ul a.selected{
  background: #B1C903;
  color: white;
}
/* #categories_block_top_sc ul a { border-bottom: none; } - I also
needed this for IE6/7 */
```

All the code that is highlighted is colors that can change the look of your navigation bar, and they are text colors and background images that you need to plan in terms of color scheme, so that the result is attractive and unique.

Footer module

You may also want to make the footer section look attractive. The next section will show how to make the footer section attractive, insert an image into it, and so on.

Time for action—Inserting an image in the footer module

The original discussion on this can be found at `http://www.PrestaShop.com/forums/viewthread/6023`.

The footer module allows us to insert images into the footer block using the back office. The maximum size of the image allowed is 307.2 KB. Format wise, you can use common image formats such as `jpg`, `png`, and `gif`.

1. Download the module file from the link at the given page.

2. Save it on your computer.

3. Upload it to your server (into your modules directory).

4. Go to your **Back Office** | **Modules** | and scroll down to **Blocks**

 For this exercise, I am using some free icons from `http://www.beautifullife.info/web-design/best-free-professional-banners/`

5. Configure the module by clicking on **>>Configure**.

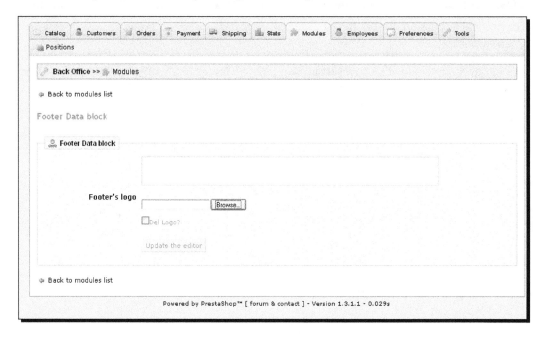

6. Insert your links into the blank field or just leave it blank.

7. Upload the **Footer's logo** or banner.

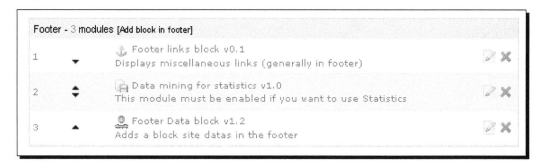

8. By default, the image will appear aligned to the left of the footer block.

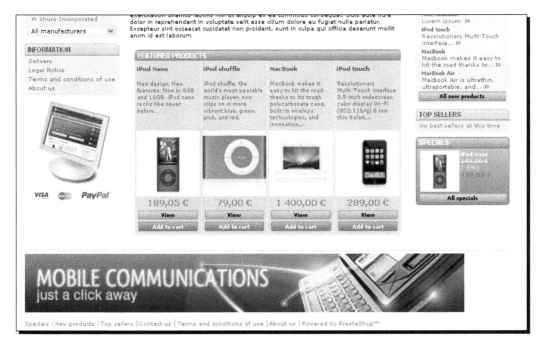

Blockfooterdata doesn't come with an external CSS file. You can insert the CSS code to align the image to the center or any way you want it.

Page peel

One of the most interesting additions to your page theme would be a page peel.

The original discussion can be found in the PrestaShop forum and you can download the module at `http://www.PrestaShop.com/forums/viewthread/28408`.

Peel page is quite interesting as the image is, in a way, hiding or peeping at the user making them curious. When a user clicks to the corner, they will be directed to a page you want to highlight or any main promotion you have.

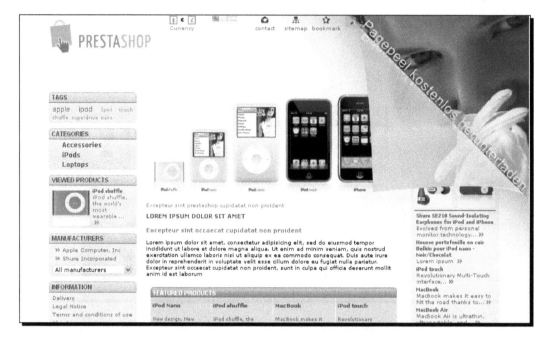

1. After you have downloaded the file, upload the file to your modules directory (/prestashop/modules/) and unzip it.

2. Go to the back office **Modules** tab (**Back Office | Modules**) and enable the installation.

3. Once you have enabled this module, you can click on **>>Configure**. This will lead you to the next screen. Insert the destination URL and upload the new image file.

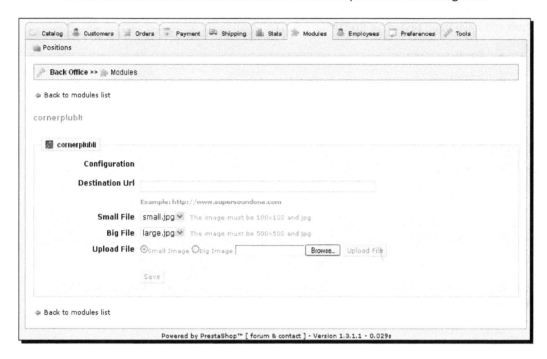

4. Click on the **Save** button when you are done.

Limitations

You can only upload `jpg` files for this module. You will need two images. The large image must be 500x500, whereas the small image must be 100x100.

You may replace the image files through the back office admin or through uploading at the modules directory `/cornerplubli.1.5/cornerplubli/images` as well.

Free third party module files used

The following are the list of the free module files used to enhance your theme. These are free and have been tested on PrestaShop 1.3.1:

- YouTube module
- jcarousels
- Gallery view
- Moving Boxes
- Horizontal top menu
- Category block on top menu
- Blockfooterdata
- Page Peels

These modules can be put into `/themes/modules` directory or the main modules directory that is `/modules/`.

For any modules to work within the `/themes/modules/` directory it has to have the following code within the module's PHP file:

```
$this->display(__FILE__, 'modulename.tpl');
```

For example, in the `blockadvertising` module folder, we have `blockadvertising.tpl` and `blockadvertising.php`.

In the `blockadvertising.php` there is a line as follows:

```
$this->display(__FILE__, 'blockadvertising.tpl');
```

You will need to work on the PHP file of each module if you want it to use the same system.

Otherwise you will have to upload the modules within the default modules folder.

This is useful to know as some third party modules may not appear or work if you put it within a theme's module folder.

Summary

In this chapter, we have explored some basic ways to add interactivity to our new PrestaShop store. We also learned how to configure the modules to enhance the look or concept of our theme.

We learned how to replace the default theme elements and insert new elements to be used within our theme.

In particular, we have covered:

- Adding a video element to the home page
- Adding `jcarousel` to feature certain items in the product lines
- Adding `jgalleryview` to showcase images on the home page
- Adding a horizontal top menu, as opposed to merely using blocks of the default modules
- Adding a winnav bar that gives better interaction to a user as he/she navigates within the PrestaShop store
- Adding the moving boxes module with more interactivity can replace the Featured Products blocks
- Adding the footer data link to enhance a webpage and add an image within the footer area
- Adding the peel element as a way to enhance certain promotions

In summary, PrestaShop gives you ample opportunities to enhance your theming tasks without difficulty. In the next chapter, you will learn about deploying your new theme.

8
Deploying Your New Themes

You have seen that creating themes in PrestaShop is much easier than most other e-commerce shopping cart sites. This is largely due to the use of the Smarty template system, which allows theme modification without requiring modification of any of the PHP files.

You are only required to modify the relevant tpl *files and most of the time deal with the* global.css *of the theme to edit the CSS.*

In this final chapter, we will go through the process of using the theme you have created and deploy it on another site. This is similar to the situation where you work within a development site and need to move or copy the theme that you have made to another site, normally a production site.

You will also go through the process of validating your themes. Although we covered this in one of the previous chapters, we will elaborate further on this aspect and underscore the importance on the web accessibility.

In order to use the new theme in another site, you will need to also consider a few factors that can be considered theme packaging conventions to help make installation of your theme as easy as possible. This is particularly useful when someone else wants to use your theme or if you are thinking about selling your new theme.

This chapter shares the final part about how to deploy a new theme. You will learn:

- ◆ How to deploy the new theme to another production site.
- ◆ How to test themes on various browsers.
- ◆ Why it is important to validate your theme.
- ◆ About the documentation that needs to be provided with the theme files.

Installing a theme on a production site

Now that you have completed the theming task, you want to use the theme in your new home or production site. If you were using your own computer as the localhost, you will have to upload these files to your new host.

Time for action—Deploying from the same host

If the theme is to be used in another domain within the same hosting, you can simply do the following:

1. Go to your server's file administration (or cPanel)

2. Find and and open the new theme folder (say, `mytheme`) from your development site (say we refer to it as domain1).

3. Copy the file `/domain1/prestashop/themes/` to your production site (for example, refer to it as domain2) at `/domain2/prestashop/themes/`.

4. Copy your `modules` directory in your development site to `/themes/ domain2/ modules/` or create a new module directory within the `mytheme` folder.

5. Go to your **Back Office | Preferences | Appearance** and select the new theme (`mytheme`) as your active theme. Click on the **Save** button.

6. Go to your front office to preview if your theme has already been applied.

7. Upload the new **Header Logo**, **Favicon**, and **Homepage logo**, as we had learned in the previous chapters.

8. Configure the module in the same way you did when you developed them through your back office **Modules** tab. By default, any new site you want to move your new theme to will have some dummy information in it. For example, **Home text editor** will have the default text **Lorem ipsum**. If your theme had those fields configured as blank, you will have to update them.

9. Check the modules enabled and transplanted on each hook through **Back Office | Modules | Positions**. Here you will see a list of hooks with the applicable modules within them. For example, you will see a hook **Right columns blocks** and a number of modules, which are transplanted in it. What this means is that those are the modules you will see in the right column in the front office.

10. If the module you need does not appear in the hook on the tab mentioned in Step 9, you will need to transplant them through **Back Office | Modules | Positions**, and click on **+Transplant a Module**. Once you transplanted the modules, you will then move them into the correct position within the hook. Some themes do not use any modules in the top block (for example, **Search**, **Language**, **Currency**, and so on) you may have to delete this from the hook.

11. Once you have done all that, preview the changes in your front office browser and validate them on different browser settings.

Time for action—Deploying from another computer

If you have been working on your localhost or an alternative server, you will need to upload these theme files to your new host. There aren't many differences in copying from within the same host.

1. Go to your server's file administration (or cPanel).

2. zip your theme directories from your localhost installation (or another host), for example, compress /yourshop1/themes/theme1 into a file called theme1.zip, which contains the theme files for theme1.

3. Upload the compressed archive to your server at /yourshop2/themes/.

4. Extract the zip file, and you should have a new theme installed. You should see the /yourshop2/themes/theme1/ folder in this directory.

5. zip your modules directory in your localhost and upload this entire directory to / themes/ theme1/modules/ or create a new module directory within the theme1 folder. Extract it so you will have the /themes/modules directory.

6. The rest of the steps would be the same as the previous one.

What just happened?

We just covered the steps required to upload your newly created theme from a local computer or another host to the new production environment.

 You must make sure the production environment is reasonably equal to your development site. It has to meet certain system requirements for PrestaShop.

Installing a third party theme "element" to your site

As much as you enjoyed creating your own theme, the time and effort to work on spectacular graphics work and the need for detailing is burdensome to many of us.

An alternative to doing everything on your own is to use one of the free themes, which resembles your desired concept, and you can cut short a lot of time and effort. There are quite a number of PrestaShop v1.2.5 themes that you can get for free instead of the latest v1.3.1. Find the one closest to your layout requirements. There are a number of basic themes at www.prestastore.com, which you can download for free.

Now, let's choose a two column theme to work with. This was developed based on the v1.2.5 platform.

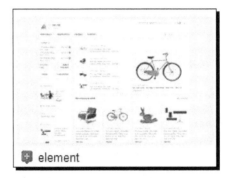

This is the preview picture of the **element** and how the main page will look when you complete the installation and deployment work.

 Although it can be used, there are some changes that have to be made to the theme files for PrestaShop v1.2.5 to ensure the correct functionalities and for you to benefit from the new upgrade of the version.

Let's move on to our next task—installing a theme to your site:

1. Download the theme file to your computer. Normally, the theme file will be named based on the name of the theme, for example, **element**.

2. Once you download the file and save it to your computer, unzip the file

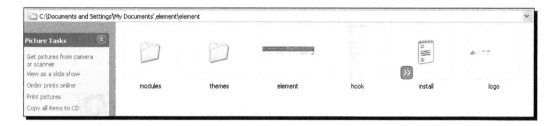

The directory of the **element** theme contains the following files and folders:

❑ modules

❑ themes

❑ hook.png

❑ install.txt

❑ logo.png

First, you can read the install.txt file to get an idea of how it works. It is a brief explanation, and you can pretty much get started using it. However, we will elaborate on how to do it in our next step.

3. zip the themes folder (which is the folder named element within the themes folder /element/themes/element/). This can be confusing for a beginner, but not to worry, if you do it incorrectly or upload the wrong folders, it will not work or will not appear on the back office **Modules** tab. Now upload this element.zip file to your server. This should go to "/yourshop/themes/"

4. Extract the themes folder on your server. You should get another new theme in your themes directory.

	Name	Size	Type
	element	4 KB	httpd/unix-directory
	mytheme	4 KB	httpd/unix-directory
	prestashop	4 KB	httpd/unix-directory
	debug.tpl	5.39 KB	text/x-generic
	element.zip	338.72 KB	package/x-generic
PHP	index.php	298 Bytes	application/x-httpd-php

5. Now, go to your **Back Office** | **Preferences** | **Appearance**, and in the **Themes** section, choose **element** to apply this theme to your site. Don't forget to click on the **Save** button.

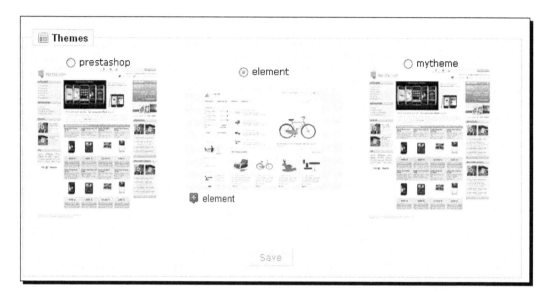

6. Remember to copy the `modules` directory `/prestashop/modules/` to your new theme folder so that you have `/themes/elements/modules` in it as shown in the next screenshot. You need to overwrite some of the modules within it with the ones we have in the computer for the theme to work as it was designed to work.

Name	Size	Type
config	4 KB	httpd/unix-directory
css	4 KB	httpd/unix-directory
img	4 KB	httpd/unix-directory
js	4 KB	httpd/unix-directory
lang	4 KB	httpd/unix-directory
modules	4 KB	httpd/unix-directory
404.tpl	787 Bytes	text/x-generic
address.tpl	5.68 KB	text/x-generic
addresses.tpl	3.14 KB	text/x-generic

If any theme you copied from the net does not work even though you copied the `modules` folder in the `themes` folder, it might not work as it does not have some code to display it correctly. You will have to copy it to the prestashop `/modules/ folder` or edit. Simplest solution is to copy the particular module folder for example, `blocktopmenu` to the default `/modules/ folder`. We also covered an alternative way in *Chapter 7, Tips and Tricks to Make PrestaShop Theming Easier*.

7. The following are the modules that you need to overwrite in previous step. If you do not see the module name in the `/theme/modules`, such as the "blocktopmenu", it is because it is a third party module that does not come by default in a PrestaShop pack.

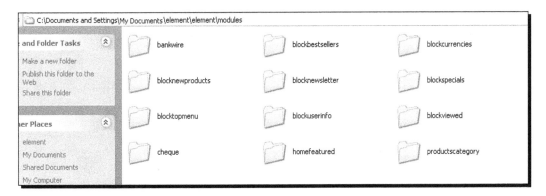

8. Check if these modules are there in **Back Office | Modules**. Enable all the modules uploaded.

Have a go hero—Transplanting the modules for the element theme.

This part is really a continuation of our previous exercise, but I have broken it into smaller chunks so that we can have more fun working on it bit-by-bit.

Now, that we have installed the theme successfully, let's work on its modules.

1. Check the `hooks.png` to see where to transplant the modules on the different blocks. This list may look pretty long, but it is not difficult to achieve. You will transplant the modules according to the list.

2. If you are not sure how to go about doing this, you may go back and refer to the sections in *Chapter 2, Customizing PrestaShop Theme Part I*, where working on modules and positioning them is covered in detail.

Time for action—Modifying the global.css for the element theme

This is the area where you need to apply what we have learned in editing CSS. As an example, you would have to modify the New Products block to make it look right in the front office.

1. Use Firebug or the Web Developer extension and check the items that require "tweaking".

2. You will know from the **Inspect Element** feature in Firebug that the New Products block is controlled by certain lines in the `global.css` file.

3. Go to `/themes/element/css` to check out the `global.css` file.

4. Go to line number 734, and edit the following line:

    ```
    /* block products (new, viewed, etc...) on left and right column
    */
      div.products_block {float:left;}
      div.products_block ul {float:right;}
    ```

5. Change it to:

    ```
    /* block products (new, viewed, etc...) on left and right column
    */
      div.products_block {float:left;}
      div.products_block ul {float:left;}
    ```

6. Then go to line number 763:

    ```
    /* Special style for block products in center column */
    #center_column .products_block{color: #595a5e; border: none;}
    #center_column .products_block h4 a {color:#ff6600; float:left }
    #center_column .products_block h3 {font-size:12px; color:black;
       padding:0.6em 0 0.6em 0.6em; margin:0 0 0.2em 0; width:645px;
       background:white; font-family:Century Gothic, Arial, Sans-Serif}
    #center_column .products_block h3 span a{float:right;
       background:url('../img/plus-detail.gif') left no-repeat;
       padding- left:1.2em; font-size:10px; text-transform:uppercase;
       margin- right:0.8em; color:#c74815; font-family:'Lucida
       Grande',Arial,sans- serif;}
    ```

```
#center_column .products_block  span{ color: #999;
   line-height:20px}
#center_column .products_block  p a {color:#666;
   font-weight:normal; font-size:11px}
#center_column .products_block  .pprice {color:black;
padding:0.2em;}
#center_column .products_block  .price_span {color:black; font-
   weight:bold; padding:0.5em 0;}
#center_column .products_block  .nav { float:right;}
#center_column .products_block  b { padding:0.1em 0.7em 0 0.7em}
#center_column .products_block  .view_it {
   background:url('../img/view_it.gif') no-repeat; width:17px;
   height:15px;}
#center_column .products_block  .add_it {
   background:url('../img/add_it.gif') no-repeat; width:17px;
   height:15px}
```

`#center_column .products_block ul li {float: left; clear: none;`
`   width:138px; margin:0.5em 1em 0.8em 0; background:white;`
`   padding:1em;}`

```
#center_column .products_block .new  {background:#98cb00;
   padding:0 0.3em 0 0.3em; position:absolute; text-align:center}
#center_column .products_block .new span  {color:white;}
#center_column .products_block .on_sale  {background:#E34514;
   padding:0 0.3em 0 0.3em; position:absolute; margin-top:2.7em;
   text- align:center}
#center_column .products_block .on_sale span  {color:white;}
```

7. Change the highlighted code to the following:

```
#center_column .products_block ul li {float: left; clear: none;
width:138px; margin:0; background:white; padding:1em;}
```

8. Now, save all the changes, and preview the theme in your front office:

You can modify the theme further according to your needs. As this theme also has a two column layout for the product page, have a look at the next screenshot to see what you have achieved:

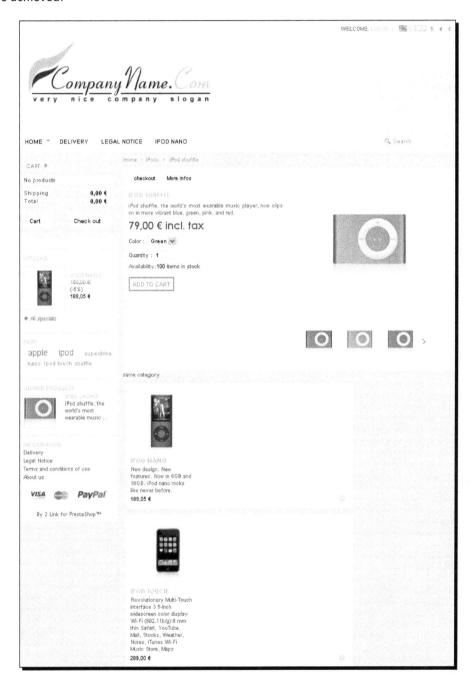

What just happened?

You successfully managed to edit the two lines from the `global.css` file to modify the theme you used! Now it is ready for public launch; you will have to make sure that the majority of users should be able to see the site, the same way you want it to be displayed. Let's go to the next section, *Checking the browser's compatibility*.

Checking the browser's compatibility

The following screenshot shows how a PrestaShop site, using the third party modules, looks in Firefox 3.5.9:

The web page using the new theme looks fine in Firefox 3.5.9. The modules which were used are viewed at the "correct" places where they are intended to appear. However, in the next screenshot, it looks pretty awkward as the right column is "pushed down" from the screen.

The modules in the center column have been pushed down to the lower areas of the web page in this browser, which is using Internet Explorer 6. This is an old version of IE. The current IE version is IE 8.

The right column has moved further down the page as well—you can't even see it without scrolling. If you have difficulty in modifying the third party modules that appear as errors in the different platform, the easiest alternative is to disable the module and replace it with another working module.

Based on our exercises for our PrestaShop theming, we have rarely touched any other files in the directory—the files which are most commonly modified are within the modules folder (those .tpl files) and within the themes folder (the global.css file). Other than that, we have learned about adding third party modules with minor changes in certain parts of the header.tpl and footer.tpl of the particular theme file.

This process of validating your web page is almost cyclical and can be best described as the following:

Write code or add new modules | Check in browsers | Check in Firebug | Check in W3C validator.

If any of the steps displays an error, you will have to restart at the point where it fails after re-editing the code or checking the third party modules.

As it is almost impossible to check every browser, the most important issue to address is which browsers do you think your audience will be using the most?

Based on statistics, the most popular web browser in 2010 is Firefox, followed by Internet Explorer 8 which is closely followed by Chrome. Firefox covers more than 4 percent of browsers usage (`http://www.w3schools.com/browsers/browsers_stats.asp`).

This simple example may have been experienced by most web designers/developers where developers have to come up with solutions to ensure that their websites are accessible by a majority, if not all, of the web users.

The interesting progression of this can be read further in a web page by Eric Meyer, who is best known for his advocacy work on behalf of web standards, most notably on CSS, a technique for managing how HTML is displayed (`http://www.ericmeyeroncss.com/bonus/render-mode.html`).

You can read more about DOCTYPE switching and the differences between rendering modes, peruse more detailed tables of DOCTYPEs, and learn what modes they trigger in which browsers at:

`http://msdn.microsoft.com/en-us/library/bb250395%28VS.85%29.aspx`

`http://www.mozilla.org/docs/web-developer/quirks/`

What validating means?

Now, what is it with W3C validators? What are they "validating"?

Basically, by combining the strengths of HTML and XML, W3C recommended a markup language that is useful now and in the future—XHTML. Through validating, we can check our documents against a Standard for various document types such as HTML, XML, and so on. This is comparable to doing proof reading of a manuscript so that it meets certain standards.

Let's step back a little and look at the various markup languages used in the web pages.

We have come across HTML, XML, and XHTML while we are looking at the files in PrestaShop.

Why validate?

The main objective of validation is to make a document "browseable" by all available platforms. We are talking about issues of accessibility. It was possible that any non-validated web was browsed, based on the capability of the error-correction in the particular browser. Unfortunately, the capability can vary between various browsers and within one browser (across various versions). Moreover, even if you know that your website looks ok in one browser, it can look totally different in another.

The same page can be displayed differently using different browsers. This is what is referred to as WYSINWOG (What You See Is Not What Others Get). Through this, the site can be used by those who are with visual disabilities and yet use the webpage without the web owner furnishing them with a separate specialized edition. As an example, most of the screen readers for visually impaired people can only be used on web pages which are made up of documents that meet those standards.

Where to validate?

There are a number of resources that can be accessed online to validate your web pages. Some are more accurate and more reliable than others.

The ones we will use as an example here are provided by the W3C, which is the international community that works to develop the standards for the World Wide Web. W3C has a number of Validation Services that include CSS validation and Mark up Validation Services. These are the free services that check conformance to W3C recommendations.

Alternatively, you can use WAVE (`http://wave.webaim.org/`), and another one that is quite popular is Cynthia Says (`http://www.cynthiasays.com/`).

WAVE will display the errors and the accessibility information of the selected page in the same page that is chosen. This way, a developer will be able to see the underlying accessibility information and make a decision on the accessibility considerations. Feedback elements are displayed through icons, which make it easier to comprehend.

Cynthia Says displays a flat report, which lists out items that do or do not comply to a developer to decide on his/her next action of his/her web page. The report is quite comprehensive and some may find it a bit complex. However, it is also a great tool to use to see if your web pages are not compliant.

The next section gives some details on the recommended standards.

XHTML

Extensible HyperText Markup Language (**XHTML**) is a combination of HTML and XML (Extensible Markup Language). XHTML is a stricter and cleaner version of HTML. XHTML is a W3C Recommendation for web pages.

It is almost identical to HTML 4.01. XHTML is HTML defined as an XML application.

XHTML 1.0 became a W3C Recommendation on January 26, 2000. XHTML is compatible with HTML 4.01. All browsers support XHTML.

The following code looks fine in a web browser:

```
<html>
  <head>
    <title>Hello World!!</title>
<body>
    <h1>Hello World!!
    <p>My new site
</body>
```

However, it is not exactly correct in terms of HTML standard rules. HTML stands for Hyper Text Markup Language, and it is not a programming language; it is a markup language. A markup language is a set of markup tags. HTML uses markup tags to describe web pages.

HTML tags are keywords surrounded by angle brackets like <html>.

These HTML tags commonly come in pairs like <p> and </p> (opening tags and closing tags respectively).

```
<html>
  <body>
    <h1>Hello World!!</h1>
    <p>My new site.</p>
  </body>
</html>
```

Web pages can still look correct even if they do not successfully validate to any specific standards. Whether they are in HTML or XHTML, they will still be displayed in the web browsers.

Based on the preceding example, the text between <html> and </html> describes the web page. The visible page content comes from the text between <body> and </body>. The text between <h1> and </h1> is displayed as a heading in a web page and the text between <p> and </p> is displayed as a paragraph in the page.

Compare the text within the following HTML tags and how it appears in a browser. You can test the code at http://www.w3schools.com/html/tryit. asp?filename=tryhtml_intro.

XML

What is XML? **eXtensible Markup Language** (**XML**) is a markup language where everything must be marked up correctly, which results in "well-formed" documents.

XML is designed to describe data, and HTML is designed to display data. It is designed to transport and store data. XML is important to know and very easy to learn.

An example of an XML file is as follows:

```
<bistro_menu>
-
  <food>
    <name>Nasi Lemak</name>
    <price>$5.95</price>
-
    <description>
      Delicious prawn sambal with deep fried crispy anchovies. Added
      withgarnishes : hard boiled eggs and sliced cucumber.
    </description>
    <calories>450</calories>
  </food>
-
  <food>
    <name>Roti Canai and Teh Tarik Happy Hours Combo</name>
    <price>$4.95</price>
-
    <description>
      Paratha served with delicious spicy curry. Together with
      "pulled tea" hot aromatic and condensed milk added to tea
      beverage. </description>
    <calories>200</calories>
  </food>
</bistro_menu>
```

XML is used in many aspects of web development, often to simplify data storage and sharing.

XML separates data from HTML, and if you need to display dynamic data in your HTML document, you will have to edit the HTML code each time the data changes.

Using XML, data is stored in separate XML files.

Through this separation, you can focus on HTML for layout and display. At the same time, any changes to the data will not require any changes to the HTML.

The validating process

You will be required to choose the type of encoding and DOCTYPE. If you are unsure, just leave the **detect automatically** on both drop-down list.

1. Validate by URL.

    Enter a URL to a web page. Don't forget to include http:// before the name of your web site. For example: http://xhtml.com/en/xhtml/reference/.

2. Validate by File Upload.

    If you are working with a static web page on your computer, you can upload it using this option.

3. Validate by Direct Input.

    This option lets you copy and paste markup from your web page into the validator.

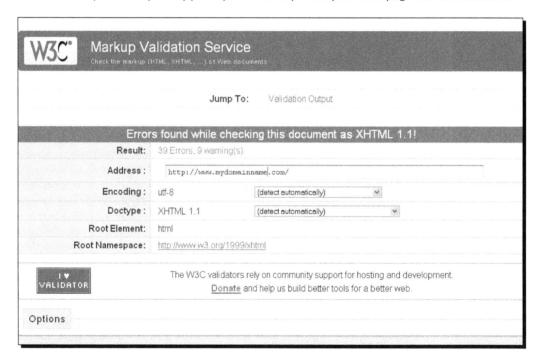

What appears as you scroll down the page will be a list of items to be checked within your PrestaShop files.

Have a go hero—Troubleshooting your new theme

Besides validating the code, there are a few simple ways to troubleshoot your new theme.

1. The image and file path must be correct. Making sure that the images are mapped according to the right image will ensure that what you plan to appear and display on the browser are written accurately; even a misspelled word can result in an "error" or no image shown on your browser.

2. Image files should be sized appropriately because there are limits to how wide they can be, as there could be conflicts with other elements. Whether you are editing the default theme or creating one from scratch, there is a possibility that your element may force the others to move down or not appear in the browser at all.

3. Syntaxes or code may be written wrongly. There are possibilities of missing brackets in your XHTML code, for example, no closing tag, tags which are inappropriately placed, or `<li>` within the wrong `<div>` tag. Different browsers, as mentioned earlier, may interpret the markup differently. Having a validation is one way to ensure that it appears the same across all browser platforms. Doing it throughout your process of adding the new code and syntaxes in your new theme is much better, as it is harder to distinguish where the errors are when you leave it to the end.

File structure of a theme

In accordance to the global standards, we need to follow certain standards or conventions in our theme development so that our work can be used by others equally well.

Your theme files should be structured the way the default PrestaShop theme does.

Your new theme directory should include the following files and folders. When you copy the default theme directory and rename it to a new name, the name of your theme will be displayed on the back office **Appearance** tab once you have it uploaded or installed on the server.

- The following folders should be present:
  - `/themes/[name of the theme]/CSS/` (files in this folder are `global.css`, `maintenance.css`, and `scene.css`).
  - `/themes/[name of the theme]/img/` (this folder consists of the `icon` folder, `jquery` folder, and a set of images used on the PrestaShop pages). This `img` directory within the theme directory provides a home for the images that are linked to the `global.css` file.
  - `/themes/[name of the theme]/js/` (the files in this folder are the `tools` folder and a set of other JavaScript files).

- ❑ /themes/[name of the theme]/lang/ (the files in this folder, by default, are fr.php and en.php).

- ◆ The following files should be located at /themes/[name of the theme]/:
  - ❑ various.tpl files relates to all the .php files in the root file of PrestaShop (for example, PrestaShop/themes/[name of the theme]/new-products.tpl will be the particular theme file for PrestaShop/new-products.php)
  - ❑ index.php file (/themes/[name of the template]/index.php)
  - ❑ /themes/[name of the template]/preview.jpg (It is the preview picture of the new theme for selection in the PrestaShop back office administration. The preview pictures are at 180x202 pixels and in the jpg format.

- ◆ You may note that the modules directory is outside the customized or new theme directory. The .tpl files for each of these modules are also within the modules directory.

- ◆ You can add another directory to the theme directory [/themes/modules], which should be copied from this /modules directory. This can be done when you want to make sure that all the modules' modifications are placed within the theme directory.

> For example, you can copy the template file from the blockbestsellers module (blockbestsellers.tpl) and place it within /themes/mynewtheme/modules/blockbestsellers.

Have a go hero—Preparing a documentation for your theme

You may find that some themes are easier to install than others. That's because there is no standard documentation required and thus, some theme designers do not provide documentation for their theme.

Since you already know how to create a theme on your own after completing the chapter, when you start working on your new themes, prepare the following.

Create a theme directory based on the name of the theme you are creating, for example, Rafflesia.

We will refer to the theme directory Rafflesia. Within this directory, you will have:

- `Installation readme`—In the `Installation readme`, briefly write all the steps. The file should be in `.txt` file format with sufficient information about your theme, author, and versions. You should provide clear instructions for the installation of the theme, but it should be concisely done. This can reside in the `/themes/` folder.

- An example can be as follows:

THEME rafflesia—PRESTASHOP 1.3.1

`http://prestashop.com`

`http://yourdomain.com`

DISTRIBUTION SOUS LICENCE CREATIVE COMMONS

`http://creativecommons.org/licenses/by-sa/2.0/fr/`

HOW TO INSTALL

----

1. Unzip the file.
2. Move the template file " rafflesia/theme/rafflesia" to "yourshop/themes".
3. Apply the template in the **Back Office | Preferences | Appearance**.
4. Replace the default PrestaShop modules by the one in the Modules `ZIP` file.
5. Verify in **Back Office | Modules** if all the modules uploaded are installed.
6. Check the `hooks.png` to see how to transplant the modules on the different blocks.
7. `Modules` folder—This folder should include all the default PrestaShop modules with their modifications and third party modules to be included in the new theme modules directory. It should reside within your site's "/themes/" folder.
8. `Theme` folders—This folder comprises `css`, `img`, `js`, and `lang` folders. It also includes all the `.tpl` files, an `index.php` file, and the preview image.
9. Preview image file—The preview image comes up after the theme is selected in the back office when you are going to apply the new theme. The size we can use should be about 180x202, which is used by default. This file resides in the "/themes/yourtheme/" folder.

10. `Additional images to preview`—It is best to provide a preview of the main landing page, the product page, and the other page of your theme if they are different from the standard default theme, so that users can preview them. Alternatively, you can provide some visual explanation on the wire frames of the new theme. This can reside within "/themes/" folder.

11. `Hooks of each modules`—an image file that shows the entire hooks of the theme.

Summary

If you have gone through the previous chapters and by the time you've reached this chapter, you must have noted that PrestaShop is one of the most powerful but the easiest and convenient solution to theming. It is a shopping cart that is robust and convenient to use, even for novice learners, as it has a very clear user interface.

In this book, you have learned that PrestaShop theming requires little effort in hardcoding and changes can easily be made without much technical knowledge. You may have come across other shopping carts which require real hard work before you get them up and running beautifully.

With PrestaShop, you simply perform a few simple steps that do not bring you any sweat at all.

This chapter concludes what you have learned previously, and in summary:

- We covered how to deploy your newly created PrestaShop theme to a production site.

- We also learned and recapped the need to check on browser compatibility throughout our theming exercise. Also, before the site is running live for public.

- We also go through the simple and fun process of installing a free theme that you can do in less than one hour.

- As you become more of an expert to theming in PrestaShop, you may want to share your new found knowledge and combine it with your design flair and creativity to make new spectacular themes for PrestaShop. You can then share your themes with other fellow PrestaShop users or be paid to create these new themes. Thus, we also covered preparing simple documentation for the theme prospective users so that they can install and use the theme easily.

In short, PrestaShop theming is a simple task even for a beginner. You can focus on your designing, and, in the end, come up with awesome and well-functioning shopping carts.

Pop Quiz–Answers

Chapter 1

Customizing PrestaShop

Pop Quiz	Answer
1	b
2	a

Chapter 2

Customizing PrestaShop Theme Part I

Pop Quiz	Answer
1	b
2	b

Chapter 5

Applying Images

Pop Quiz	Answer
1	background-position: 5cm 10cm
2	background-position: 25% 50%
3	background-position: top left

Chapter 7

Tips and Trick to Make Prestashop Theme Easier

Pop Quiz	Answer
1	a
2	b

Index

I

icons
  default icons replacing, another icon
      set used 181
  replacing 179
  replacing, own icon set used 182
  selected icons, replacing 179, 180
images
  in blocks, replacing 171, 172
  inserting, in footer module 257, 258
img folder 198
Installation readme 285
installing, theme
  on production site 266
installing, third party theme element 268-271

J

jcarousel 232
jcarousel modules 232
jgalleryview module dimension
  modifying 244
jQuery 218, 219
jQuery plug-in 232

K

key elements 61
key module blocks 59
keywords 280

L

languages block 70
layout
  main pages, modifying 200
logo
  about 63
  adding 174
  online resources 63, 64
  replacing, header.tpl file used 174, 175
  replacing, on site 64, 65

M

maintenance.css
  about 100

content 100, 101
  ID selectors 101
  maintenance, ID selectors 101
  maintenance.tpl file 102
  message, ID selectors 101
  message.image, ID selectors 101
maintenance mode screen
  modifying 103-105
MANUFACTURERS block
  header text color, changing 131, 132
Model-View-Controller architecture. *See* MVC
    architecture
module blocks, footer.tpl
  modifying 210
module files
  third party 262
modules
  enabling 41, 42
  installing 41, 42
  moving, within column 50
  on page, configuring 57, 58
  selecting, to install 42, 43
modules block
  block names, modifying 91, 92
modules folder 198
modules, PrestaShop 1.3.1
  advertisement 40
  blocks 40
  payment 40
  products 40
  stats 40
  stats engine 40
  tools 40
modules tab, back office administration panel
  about 26, 39-41
  modules, enabling 41, 42
  modules, installing 41, 42
  modules, positioning 43
  modules, selecting to install 42, 43
modules, third party theme element
  transplanting 271
modules, transplanting
  about 44
  blocks, adding 46
  blocks, moving 50-53
  CART, shifting to top position 54
  Categories block, configuring 48, 49

Thank you for buying
PrestaShop 1.3 Theming Beginner's Guide

About Packt Publishing

Packt, pronounced 'packed', published its first book "*Mastering phpMyAdmin for Effective MySQL Management*" in April 2004 and subsequently continued to specialize in publishing highly focused books on specific technologies and solutions.

Our books and publications share the experiences of your fellow IT professionals in adapting and customizing today's systems, applications, and frameworks. Our solution based books give you the knowledge and power to customize the software and technologies you're using to get the job done. Packt books are more specific and less general than the IT books you have seen in the past. Our unique business model allows us to bring you more focused information, giving you more of what you need to know, and less of what you don't.

Packt is a modern, yet unique publishing company, which focuses on producing quality, cutting-edge books for communities of developers, administrators, and newbies alike. For more information, please visit our website: www.packtpub.com.

About Packt Open Source

In 2010, Packt launched two new brands, Packt Open Source and Packt Enterprise, in order to continue its focus on specialization. This book is part of the Packt Open Source brand, home to books published on software built around Open Source licences, and offering information to anybody from advanced developers to budding web designers. The Open Source brand also runs Packt's Open Source Royalty Scheme, by which Packt gives a royalty to each Open Source project about whose software a book is sold.

Writing for Packt

We welcome all inquiries from people who are interested in authoring. Book proposals should be sent to author@packtpub.com. If your book idea is still at an early stage and you would like to discuss it first before writing a formal book proposal, contact us; one of our commissioning editors will get in touch with you.

We're not just looking for published authors; if you have strong technical skills but no writing experience, our experienced editors can help you develop a writing career, or simply get some additional reward for your expertise.

[PACKT] open source *
PUBLISHING
community experience distilled

Learn by doing: less theory, more results

PrestaShop 1.3

Build and customize your online store with this
speedy, lightweight e-commerce solution

Beginner's Guide

John Horton   [   ] open source

PrestaShop 1.3 Beginner's Guide

ISBN: 978-1-849511-14-8   Paperback: 308 pages

Build and customize your online store with this
speedy, lightweight e-commerce solution

1. Covers every topic required to start and run
   a real, trading e-commerce business with
   PrestaShop.

2. Deploy PrestaShop quickly and easily, and
   make your PrestaShop search-engine friendly.

3. Learn how to turn a single new PrestaShop into
   a thriving e-commerce empire.

4. Step-by-step fully illustrated explanation and
   discussions aimed at helping beginners like you
   towards the realization of your own PrestaShop
   store and beyond.

Learn by doing: less theory, more results

Moodle 1.9
Theme Design

Customize the appearance of your Moodle Theme
by using Moodle's powerful theming engine

Beginner's Guide

Paul James Gadsdon   [   ] open source

Moodle 1.9 Theme Design: Beginner's Guide

ISBN: 978-1-849510-14-1   Paperback: 308 pages

Customize the appearance of your Moodle Theme
using its powerful theming engine

1. Create your own Moodle theme from the
   graphic design stage right through to the
   finished complete Moodle theme.

2. Offers design examples and ways to create
   appropriate themes for different student age
   groups and styles.

3. Effective planning for creating and modifying
   new themes, customizing existing themes, and
   enhancing them further.

Please check **www.PacktPub.com** for information on our titles

Magento 1.3 Theme Design

ISBN: 978-1-847196-64-4   Paperback: 188 pages

Customize the appearance of your Magento
e-commerce store with Magento's powerful
theming engine

1. Give your Magento stores a unique branded
    look and feel by creating your own Magento
    themes.

2. Use design techniques to reinforce your brand
    message and increase sales.

3. Customise your Magento theme's look, feel,
    layout, and features.

Drupal 5 Views Recipes

ISBN: 978-1-847196-96-5   Paperback: 412 pages

94 recipes to develop custom content displays for
your Drupal web site

1. Display particular types of content in unique
    and compelling ways on your Drupal web site.

2. Enhance your web site with calendars,
    timelines, galleries, maps, podcasts, Views
    Fusion, and more.

3. Indispensable resources for Drupal 5
    Administrators – Drupal Administration Menu,
    Views Bulk Operations, ModuleInfo, and
    Editable Fields modules.

www.ingramcontent.com/pod-product-compliance
Lightning Source LLC
Chambersburg PA
CBHW062108050326
40690CB00016B/3249